A LOVE WORTH GIVING

OTHER BOOKS BY MAX LUCADO

Inspirational

A Gentle Thunder
A Love Worth Giving
And the Angels Were Silent
Come Thirsty
Cure for the Common Life
God Came Near
He Chose the Nails
He Still Moves Stones
In the Eye of the Storm
In the Grip of Grace
It's Not about Me
Just Like Jesus
Next Door Savior
No Wonder They Call Him the Savior
On the Anvil
Six Hours One Friday
The Applause of Heaven
The Great House of God
Traveling Light
When Christ Comes
When God Whispers Your Name

Children's Books

Alabaster's Song
All You Ever Need
Because I Love You
Flo the Lyin' Fly
He Chose You
Hermie, a Common Caterpillar
If Only I Had a Green Nose
Jacob's Gift
Just in Case You Ever Wonder
Just Like Jesus (for teens)
Just the Way You Are
Next Door Savior (for teens)
*Punchinello
and the Most Marvelous Gift*

Small Gifts in God's Hands
Tell Me the Secrets
Tell Me the Story
The Crippled Lamb
The Way Home
Webster the Scaredy Spider
With You All the Way
You Are Mine
You Are Special

Gift Books

America Looks Up
Everyday Blessings
God's Inspirational Promises
God Thinks You're Wonderful
Grace for the Moment
Grace for the Moment Journal
In the Footsteps of Jesus
Just for You
Just Like Jesus Devotional
Let the Journey Begin
Mocha with Max
One Incredible Moment
Safe in the Shepherd's Arms
The Cross
The Gift for All People
The Greatest Moments
Traveling Light for Mothers
Traveling Light Journal
Turn
Walking with the Savior

Fiction

An Angel's Story
The Christmas Child

A
LOVE
WORTH
GIVING

LIVING *in the* OVERFLOW
of GOD'S LOVE

MAX LUCADO

W PUBLISHING GROUP
A Division of Thomas Nelson Publishers
Since 1798
www.wpublishinggroup.com

Published by W Publishing Group, a Division of Thomas Nelson, Inc., P.O. Box 141000, Nashville, Tennessee 37214.

W Publishing Group books may be purchased in bulk for educational, business, fund-raising, or sales promotional use. For information, please e-mail SpecialMarkets@ThomasNelson.com.

Unless otherwise noted, Scripture quotations used in this book are from the Holy Bible, New Century Version, copyright © 1987, 1988, 1991 by Word Publishing, Dallas, Texas 75234. Used by permission. Other Scripture references are from the following sources: The Contemporary English Version (CEV), © 1991, 1992, 1995 by the American Bible Society. Used by permission. The Holy Bible, English Standard Version (ESV), copyright © 2001 by Crossway Bibles, a division of Good News Publishers. Used by permission. All rights reserved. The Jerusalem Bible (JB) © 1966, 1967, 1968 by Darton, Longman & Todd, Ltd. and Doubleday. The Living Bible (TLB) copyright © 1971 by Tyndale House Publishers, Inc., Wheaton, Illinois 60189. Used by permission. The Message (MSG), copyright © by Eugene H. Peterson 1993, 1994, 1995. Used by permission of NavPress Publishing Group. The New American Standard Bible® (NASB) © 1960, 1962, 1963, 1968, 1971, 1972, 1973, 1975, 1977, 1995 by The Lockman Foundation. Used by permission. (www.Lockman.org). The New English Bible (NEB) copyright © 1961, 1970 by the Delegates of the Oxford University Press and the Syndics of the Cambridge University Press. The Holy Bible, New International Version®. NIV® (NIV). Copyright © 1973, 1978, 1984 by the International Bible Society. Used by permission of Zondervan Publishing House. The New King James Version (NKJV), copyright © 1979, 1980, 1982 by Thomas Nelson, Inc., Publishers. The Holy Bible, New Living Translation (NLT), copyright © 1996. Used by permission of Tyndale House Publishers, Inc., Wheaton, Illinois 60189. All rights reserved. J. B. Phillips: The New Testament in Modern English, Revised Edition (PHILLIPS). Copyright © by J. B. Phillips 1958, 1960, 1972, 1986, 1988. The Revised Standard Version of the Bible (RSV), copyright © 1946, 1952, and 1971 by the Division of Christian Education of the National Council of the Churches of Christ in the USA. The Good News Bible: The Bible in Today's English Version, Second Edition (TEV). Copyright © 1992 by the American Bible Society.

Library of Congress Cataloging-in-Publication data

Lucado, Max.
   A love worth giving : living in the overflow of God's love / by Max Lucado.
      p. cm.
Includes bibliographical references.
   ISBN 0-8499-1346-2 (tp)
   ISBN 0-8499-1759-X (hc)
   1. God—Love. 2. Love—Religious aspects—Christianity. 3. Christian life. I. Title.
   BT140 .L83 2002
   231'.6—dc21   2002008238

Printed in the United States of America
06 07 08 09 10 RRD 9 8 7 6 5 4 3

To my daughter Jenna on her eighteenth birthday.
A higher joy and deeper pride no father could know.
I love you.

CONTENTS

~⊙

ACKNOWLEDGMENTS

The fingerprints of many dear ones are on these pages.

Liz Heaney and Karen Hill—Your patience is exceeded only by your skill. Thanks for the brilliant editing.

Steve and Cheryl Green—Can you believe it? Three decades of friendship! Thanks for keeping this ship on course.

Susan Perry—Thanks for the sweet spirit you add to our office.

The Oak Hills Church of Christ—We're living in an era of answered prayer. And you are the answer to one of mine.

The "W" team—You're not just my publishers; you're my family.

Carol Bartley and Laura Kendall—For the constellation of corrections you gave this manuscript, I'm in your debt.

Charles Shinn—Prayer partner, golf buddy, shepherd, and just all-around good guy. Thanks for showing up.

Charles Prince—Gentleman scholar and dear adviser.

Steve Halliday—Your discussion guide is terrific! Thanks for another great job.

Jenna, Andrea, and Sara—You make other dads jealous and this dad beam. I love you.

Denalyn—A guy could get lost in your brown eyes.

To you, the reader—May you find a love worth giving.

And to you, our heavenly Father—Can an ocean be captured in a thimble? Can the tone deaf play Mozart? Can a mouse understand the majesty of the Rocky Mountains? Of course not. And can any words capture your love? By no means. But what joy is found in the attempt.

THE 7:47 PRINCIPLE

We love, because He first loved us.

1 JOHN 4:19 NASB

GOD LOVES YOU. PERSONALLY. POWERFULLY. PASSIONATELY.

OTHERS HAVE PROMISED AND FAILED.

BUT GOD HAS PROMISED AND SUCCEEDED.

HE LOVES YOU WITH AN UNFAILING LOVE.

AND HIS LOVE—IF YOU WILL LET IT—CAN FILL YOU

AND LEAVE YOU WITH A LOVE WORTH GIVING.

Could two people be more different?

He is looked up to. She is looked down on.

He is a church leader. She is a streetwalker.

He makes a living promoting standards. She's made a living breaking them.

He's hosting the party. She's crashing it.

Ask the other residents of Capernaum to point out the more pious of the two, and they'll pick Simon. Why, after all, he's a student of theology, a man of the cloth. Anyone would pick him. Anyone, that is, except Jesus. Jesus knew them both. And Jesus would pick the woman. Jesus does pick the woman. And, what's more, he tells Simon why.

Not that Simon wants to know. His mind is elsewhere. *How did this whore get in my house?* He doesn't know whom to yell at first, the woman or the servant who let her in. After all, this dinner is a formal affair. Invitation only. Upper crust. Crème de la crème. Who let the riffraff in?

Simon is angry. *Just look at her—groveling at Jesus' feet. Kissing them, no less! Why, if Jesus were who he says he is, he would have nothing to do with this woman.*

One of the lessons Simon learned that day was this: Don't think thoughts you don't want Jesus to hear. For Jesus heard them, and when he did, he chose to share a few of his own.

> "Simon," he said to the Pharisee, "I have something to say to you."
> "All right, Teacher," Simon replied, "go ahead."
> Then Jesus told him this story: "A man loaned money to two people—five hundred pieces of silver to one and fifty pieces to the other. But neither of them could repay him, so he kindly forgave them both, canceling their debts. Who do you suppose loved him more after that?"
> Simon answered, "I suppose the one for whom he canceled the larger debt."
> "That's right," Jesus said. Then he turned to the woman and said to Simon, "Look at this woman kneeling here. When I entered your home, you didn't offer me water to wash the dust from my feet, but she has washed them with her tears and wiped them with her hair. You didn't give me a kiss of greeting, but she has kissed my feet again and again from the time I first came in. You neglected the courtesy of olive oil to anoint my head, but she has anointed my feet with rare perfume. I tell you, her sins—and they are many—have been forgiven, so she has shown me much love. But a person who is forgiven little shows only little love." (Luke 7:40–47 NLT)

Simon invites Jesus to his house but treats him like an unwanted step-uncle. No customary courtesies. No kiss of greeting. No washing his feet. No oil for his head.

Or, in modern terms, no one opened the door for him, took his coat, or shook his hand. Count Dracula has better manners.

Simon does nothing to make Jesus feel welcome. The woman, however, does everything that Simon didn't. We aren't told her name. Just her reputation—a sinner. A prostitute most likely. She has no invitation to the party and no standing in the community. (Imagine a hooker in a tight dress showing up at the parsonage during the pastor's Christmas party. Heads turn. Faces blush. Gasp!)

But people's opinions didn't stop her from coming. It's not for them she has come. It's for him. Her every move is measured and meaningful. Each gesture extravagant. She puts her cheek to his feet, still dusty from the path. She has no water, but she has tears. She has no towel, but she has her hair. She uses both to bathe the feet of Christ. As one translation reads, "she rained tears" on his feet (v. 44 MSG). She opens a vial of perfume, perhaps her only possession of worth, and massages it into his skin. The aroma is as inescapable as the irony.

You'd think Simon of all people would show such love. Is he not the reverend of the church, the student of Scripture? But he is harsh, distant. You'd think the woman would avoid Jesus. Is she not the woman of the night, the town hussy? But she can't resist him. Simon's "love" is calibrated and stingy. Her love, on the other hand, is extravagant and risky.

How do we explain the difference between the two? Training? Education? Money? No, for Simon has outdistanced her in all three.

But there is one area in which the woman leaves him eating dust. Think about it. What one discovery has she made that Simon hasn't? What one treasure does she cherish that Simon doesn't? Simple. God's love. We don't know when she received it. We aren't told how she heard about it. Did she overhear Jesus' words "Your Father is merciful" (Luke 6:36 ESV)? Was she nearby when Jesus had compassion on the widow of Nain? Did someone tell her how Jesus touched lepers and turned tax collectors into disciples? We don't know. But we know this. She came thirsty. Thirsty from guilt. Thirsty from regret. Thirsty from countless nights of making love and finding none. She came thirsty.

And when Jesus hands her the goblet of grace, she drinks. She doesn't just taste or nip. She doesn't dip her finger and lick it or take the cup and sip it. She lifts the liquid to her lips and drinks, gulping and swallowing like the parched pilgrim she is. She drinks until the mercy flows down her chin and onto her neck and chest. She drinks until every inch of her soul is moist and soft. She comes thirsty and she drinks. She drinks deeply.

Simon, on the other hand, doesn't even know he is thirsty. People like Simon don't need grace; they analyze it. They don't request mercy; they debate and prorate it. It wasn't that Simon couldn't be forgiven; he just never asks to be.

So while she drinks up, he puffs up. While she has ample love to give, he has no love to offer. Why? The 7:47 Principle. Read again verse 47 of chapter 7: "A person who is forgiven little shows only little love." Just like the jumbo jet, the 7:47 Principle has wide wings. Just like the aircraft, this truth can lift you to another level. Read it one more time. "A person who is forgiven little shows only little love." In other words, we can't give what we've never received. If we've never received love, how can we love others?

But, oh, how we try! As if we can conjure up love by the sheer force of will. As if there is within us a distillery of affection that lacks only a piece of wood or a hotter fire. We poke it and stoke it with resolve. What's our typical strategy for treating a troubled relationship? Try harder.

"My spouse needs my forgiveness? I don't know how, but I'm going to give it."

"I don't care how much it hurts, I'm going to be nice to that bum."

"I'm supposed to love my neighbor? Okay. By golly, I will."

So we try. Teeth clinched. Jaw firm. We're going to love if it kills us! And it may do just that.

Could it be we are missing a step? Could it be that the first step of love is not toward them but toward him? Could it be that the secret to loving is receiving? You give love by first receiving it. "We love, because he first loved us" (1 John 4:19 NASB).

Long to be more loving? Begin by accepting your place as a dearly loved child. "Be imitators of God, therefore, as dearly loved children and live a life of love, just as Christ loved us" (Eph. 5:1–2 NIV).

Want to learn to forgive? Then consider how you've been forgiven. "Be kind and compassionate to one another, forgiving each other, just as in Christ God forgave you" (Eph. 4:32 NIV).

Finding it hard to put others first? Think of the way Christ put you first. "Though he was God, he did not demand and cling to his rights as God" (Phil. 2:6 NLT).

Need more patience? Drink from the patience of God (2 Pet. 3:9). Is generosity an elusive virtue? Then consider how generous God has been with you (Rom. 5:8). Having trouble putting up with ungrateful relatives or cranky neighbors? God puts up with you when you act the same. "He is kind to the ungrateful and wicked" (Luke 6:35 NIV).

Can't we love like this?

Not without God's help we can't. Oh, we may succeed for a time. We, like Simon, may open a door. But our relationships need more than a social gesture. Some of our spouses need a foot washing. A few of our friends need a flood of tears. Our children need to be covered in the oil of our love.

But if we haven't received these things ourselves, how can we give them to others? Apart from God, "the heart is deceitful above all things" (Jer. 17:9 NIV). A marriage-saving love is not within us. A friendship-preserving devotion cannot be found in our hearts. We need help from an outside source. A transfusion. Would we love as God loves? Then we start by receiving God's love.

We preachers have been guilty of skipping the first step. "Love each other!" we tell our churches. "Be patient, kind, forgiving," we urge. But instructing people to love without telling them they are loved is like telling them to write a check without our making a deposit in their accounts. No wonder so many relationships are overdrawn. Hearts have insufficient love. The apostle John models the right sequence. He makes a deposit before he tells us to write the check. First, the deposit:

> God showed how much he loved us by sending his only Son into the world so that we might have eternal life through him. This is real love. It is not that we loved God, but that he loved us and sent his Son as a sacrifice to take away our sins. (1 John 4:9–10 NLT)

And then, having made such an outrageous, eye-opening deposit, John calls on you and me to pull out the checkbook: "Dear friends, since God loved us that much, we surely ought to love each other" (v. 11 NLT).

The secret to loving is living loved. This is the forgotten first step in relationships. Remember Paul's prayer? "May your roots go down deep into the soil of God's marvelous love" (Eph. 3:17 NLT). As a tree draws nutrients from the soil, we draw nourishment from the Father. But what if the tree has no contact with the soil?

I was thinking of this yesterday as I disassembled our Christmas tree. That's my traditional New Year's Day chore. Remove the ornaments, carry out the tree, and sweep up all the needles. There are thousands of them! The tree is falling apart. Blame it on bad rooting. For two weeks this tree has been planted in a metal bowl. What comes from a tree holder?

Old Simon had the same problem. Impressive to look at, nicely decorated, but he falls apart when you give him a shove or two.

Sound familiar? Does bumping into certain people leave you brittle, breakable, and fruitless? Do you easily fall apart? If so, your love may be grounded in the wrong soil. It may be rooted in their love (which is fickle) or in your resolve to love (which is frail). John urges us to "rely on the love *God* has for us" (1 John 4:16 NIV, emphasis mine). He alone is the power source.

Many people tell us to love. Only God gives us the power to do so.

We know what God wants us to do. "This is what God commands: . . . that we love each other" (1 John 3:23). But how can we? How can we be kind to the vow breakers? To those who are unkind to us? How can we be patient with people who have the warmth of a vulture and the tenderness of a porcupine? How can we forgive the moneygrubbers and backstabbers we meet, love, and marry? How can we love as God loves? We want to. We long to. But how can we?

By living loved. By following the 7:47 Principle: Receive first, love second.

Want to give it a try? Let's carry this principle up the Mount Everest of love writings. More than one person has hailed 1 Corinthians 13 as the finest chapter in the Bible. No words get to the heart of loving people like these verses. And no verses get to the heart of the chapter like verses 4 through 8.

> Love is patient, love is kind. It does not envy, it does not boast, it is not proud. It is not rude, it is not self-seeking, it is not easily angered, it keeps no record of wrongs. Love does not delight in evil but rejoices with the truth. It always protects, always trusts, always hopes, always perseveres. Love never fails. (NIV)

Several years ago someone challenged me to replace the word *love* in this passage with my name. I did and became a liar. "Max is patient, Max is kind. Max does not envy, he does not boast, he is not proud. . . ." That's enough! Stop right there! Those words are false. Max is not patient. Max is not kind. Ask my wife and kids. Max can be an out-and-out clod! That's my problem.

And for years that was my problem with this paragraph. It set a standard I could not meet. No one can meet it. No one, that is, except Christ. Does this passage not describe the measureless love of God? Let's insert Christ's name in place of the word *love,* and see if it rings true.

> Jesus is patient, Jesus is kind. Jesus does not envy, he does not boast, he is not proud. Jesus is not rude, he is not self-seeking, he is not easily angered, he keeps no record of wrongs. Jesus does not delight in evil but rejoices with the truth. Jesus always protects, always trusts, always hopes, always perseveres. Jesus never fails.

Rather than let this scripture remind us of a love we cannot produce, let it remind us of a love we cannot resist—God's love.

Some of you are so thirsty for this type of love. Those who should have loved you didn't. Those who could have loved you didn't. You were left at the hospital. Left at the altar. Left with an empty bed. Left with a broken heart. Left with your question "Does anybody love me?"

Please listen to heaven's answer. God loves you. Personally. Powerfully. Passionately. Others have promised and failed. But God has promised and succeeded. He loves you with an unfailing love. And his love—if you will let it—can fill you and leave you with a love worth giving.

So come. Come thirsty and drink deeply.

CHAPTER TWO

Love's Flagship

Love is patient.

1 Corinthians 13:4

PATIENCE IS THE RED CARPET UPON WHICH
GOD'S GRACE APPROACHES US.

See the people hiding in the house? That's us. The folks ducking behind the stairwell? That's you and me. We're avoiding the bill collectors. This is the eve of eviction. The bank has given us one day to pay the mortgage. Credit-card agents are camped on the front lawn. Loan sharks have our number on speed dial. But we are broke. We've peddled our last food stamp. The water is disconnected, the car repossessed, the furniture picked up, and now the IRS agent is knocking on the door. He wants back taxes. "I know you are in there. Open up!"

So we do. He tells us how much we owe; we remind him that turnips give no blood. He mentions jail, and at this point a warm bed out of the reach of creditors doesn't sound half bad.

Just as he motions for the sheriff, his cell phone rings. It's Washington. The president wants a word with us, an explanation from us. We have none. No defense. Only a plea for patience. He listens in silence and asks to speak with the agent again. As the president speaks, the suit nods and says, "Yessir . . . Yessir . . . Yessir." He closes his phone and looks first at you and then at me. "I don't know who you know, but your debt is paid," he says, tearing up the papers and letting the pieces fall.

Maybe you didn't know God did that for us. Maybe no one has told you about "God's . . . patience and willingness to put up with you" (Rom. 2:4 CEV). Could be you dozed off the day the minister read Psalm 103:8: "The LORD is compassionate and gracious, slow to anger, abounding in love" (NIV). If so, no wonder you've been edgy. No wonder you've been impatient. Bankruptcy can put the best of us in a foul mood. You know what you need to do?

Step out on the porch. Stand where the IRS guy stood, and look at those papers—the torn pieces scattered and strewn across the lawn. Stare at the proof of God's patience.

You were in debt!

Those times you used his name only when you cussed? God could have blown up at you. But he didn't. He was patient.

Those thousand sunsets you never thanked him for? He could have put you on beauty rations. But he didn't. He was patient with you.

Those Sundays you strutted into church to show off the new dress? It's a wonder he didn't strike you naked. But he didn't. He was patient.

And, oh my, those promises: "Get me out of this, and I'll never tell another lie." "Count on me to stand up for you from now on." "I'm done with temper tantrums, Lord." Goodness gracious. If broken promises were lumber, we could build a subdivision. Doesn't God have ample reason to walk out on us?

But he doesn't. Why? Because "God is being patient with you" (2 Pet. 3:9).

Paul presents patience as the premiere expression of love. Positioned at the head of the apostle's Love Armada—a boat-length or two in front of kindness, courtesy, and forgiveness—is the flagship known as patience. "Love is patient" (1 Cor. 13:4).

The Greek word used here for *patience* is a descriptive one. It figuratively means "taking a long time to boil." Think about a pot of boiling water. What factors determine the speed at which it boils? The size of the stove? No. The pot? The utensil may have an influence, but the primary factor is the intensity of the flame. Water boils quickly when the flame is high. It boils slowly when the flame is low. Patience "keeps the burner down."

Helpful clarification, don't you think? Patience isn't naive. It doesn't ignore misbehavior. It just keeps the flame low. It waits. It listens. It's slow to boil. This is how God treats us. And, according to Jesus, this is how we should treat others.

He once told a parable about a king who decides to settle his accounts with his debtors. His bookkeeper surfaces a fellow who owes not thousands or hundreds of thousands but millions of dollars. The king summarily declares that the man and his wife and kids are to be sold to pay the debt. Because of his inability to pay, the man is about to lose everything and everyone dear to him. No wonder

> the man fell down before the king and begged him, "Oh, sir, be *patient* with me, and I will pay it all." Then the king was filled with pity for him, and he released him and forgave his debt. (Matt. 18:26–27 NLT, emphasis mine)

The word *patience* makes a surprise appearance here. The debtor does not plead for mercy or forgiveness; he pleads for patience. Equally curious is this singular appearance of the word. Jesus uses it twice in this story and never again. It appears nowhere else in the Gospels. Perhaps the scarce usage is the first-century equivalent of a highlighter. Jesus reserves the word for one occasion to make one point. Patience is more than a virtue for long lines and slow waiters. Patience is the red carpet upon which God's grace approaches us.

Had there been no patience, there would have been no mercy. But the king was patient, and the man with the multimillion-dollar debt was forgiven.

But then the story takes a left turn. The freshly forgiven fellow makes a beeline from the courthouse to the suburbs. There he searches out a guy who owes him some money.

> But when the man left the king, he went to a fellow servant who owed him a few thousand dollars. He grabbed him by the throat and demanded instant payment. His fellow servant fell down before him and begged for a little more time. "Be *patient* and I will pay it," he pleaded. But his creditor wouldn't wait. He had the man arrested and jailed until the debt could be paid in full. (vv. 28–30 NLT, emphasis mine)

The king is stunned. How could the man be so impatient? How *dare* the man be so impatient! The ink of the CANCELED stamp is still moist on the man's bills. Wouldn't you expect a little Mother Teresa–ness out of him? You'd think that a person who'd been forgiven so much would love much. But he didn't. And his lack of love led to a costly mistake.

The unforgiving servant is called back to the castle.

> "You evil servant!" [the king, a.k.a. God, declares.] "I forgave you that tremendous debt because you pleaded with me. Shouldn't you have mercy on your fellow servant, just as I had mercy on you?" Then the angry king sent the man to prison until he had paid every penny. (Matt. 18:32–34 NLT)

The king's patience made no difference in the man's life. To the servant, throne-room mercy was nothing more than a canceled test, a dodged bullet, a get-out-of-jail-free card. He wasn't stunned by the royal grace; he was relieved he hadn't been punished. He was given much patience but gave none, which makes us wonder if he actually understood the gift he had received.

If you find patience hard to give, you might ask the same question. How infiltrated are you with God's patience? You've heard about it. Read about it. Perhaps underlined Bible passages regarding it. But have you received it? The proof is in your patience. Patience deeply received results in patience freely offered.

But patience never received leads to an abundance of problems, not the least of which is prison. Remember where the king sent the unforgiving servant? "Then the angry king sent the man to prison until he had paid every penny" (Matt. 18:34 NLT).

Whew! we sigh. *Glad that story is a parable. It's a good thing God doesn't imprison the impatient in real life.* Don't be so sure he doesn't. Self-absorption and ingratitude make for thick walls and lonely jails.

Impatience still imprisons the soul. For that reason, our God is quick to help us avoid it. He does more than demand patience from us; he offers it to us. Patience is a fruit of his Spirit. It hangs from the tree of Galatians 5:22: "The Spirit produces the fruit of love, joy, peace, patience." Have you asked God to give you some fruit? *Well I did once, but . . .* But what? Did you, h'm, grow impatient? Ask him again and again and again. He won't grow impatient with your pleading, and you will receive patience in your praying.

And while you're praying, ask for understanding. "Patient people have great understanding" (Prov. 14:29). Could it be your impatience stems from a lack of understanding? Mine has.

Sometime ago our church staff attended a leadership conference. Especially interested in one class, I arrived early and snagged a front-row seat. As the speaker began, however, I was distracted by a couple of voices in the back of the room. Two guys were mumbling to each other. I was giving serious thought to shooting a glare over my shoulder when the speaker offered an explanation. "Forgive me," he said. "I forgot to explain why the two fellows at the back of the class are talking. One of them is an elder at a new church in Romania. He has traveled here to learn about church leadership. But he doesn't speak English, so the message is being translated."

All of a sudden everything changed. Patience replaced impatience. Why? Because patience always hitches a ride with understanding. The wise man says, "A man of understanding holds his tongue" (Prov. 11:12 NIV). He also says, "A man of understanding is even-tempered" (Prov. 17:27 NIV). Don't miss the connection between understanding and patience. Before you blow up, listen up. Before you strike out, tune in. "It takes wisdom to have a good family, and it takes understanding to make it strong" (Prov. 24:3).

Before anything else, love is patient.

For an example, come with me to Paris, France, 1954. Elie Wiesel is a correspondent for a Jewish newspaper. A decade earlier he was a prisoner in a Jewish concentration camp. A decade later he would be known as the author of *Night*, the Pulitzer Prize–winning account of the Holocaust. Eventually he'll be awarded the Congressional Medal of Achievement and the Nobel Peace Prize.

But tonight Elie Wiesel is a twenty-six-year-old unknown newspaper correspondent. He is about to interview the French author François Mauriac, who is a devout Christian. Mauriac is France's most recent Nobel laureate for literature and an expert on French political life.

Wiesel shows up at Mauriac's apartment, nervous and chain-smoking— his emotions still frayed from the German horror, his comfort as a writer still raw. The older Mauriac tries to put him at ease. He invites Wiesel in, and the two sit in the small room. Before Wiesel can ask a question, however, Mauriac, a staunch Roman Catholic, begins to speak about his favorite subject: Jesus. Wiesel grows uneasy. The name of Jesus is a pressed thumb on his infected wounds.

Wiesel tries to reroute the conversation but can't. It is as though everything in creation leads back to Jesus. Jerusalem? Jerusalem is where Jesus ministered. The Old Testament? Because of Jesus, the Old is now enriched by the New. Mauriac turns every topic toward the Messiah. The anger in Wiesel begins to heat. The Christian anti-Semitism he'd grown up with, the layers of grief from Sighet, Auschwitz, and Buchenwald—it all boils over. He puts away his pen, shuts his notebook, and stands up angrily.

"Sir," he said to the still-seated Mauriac, "you speak of Christ. Christians love to speak of him. The passion of Christ, the agony of Christ, the death of Christ. In your religion, that is all you speak of. Well, I want you to know that ten years ago, not very far from here, I knew Jewish children every one of whom suffered a thousand times more, six million times more, than Christ on the cross. And we don't speak about them. Can you understand that, sir? We don't speak about them."[1]

Mauriac is stunned. Wiesel turns and marches out the door. Mauriac sits in shock, his woolen blanket still around him. The young reporter is pressing the elevator button when Mauriac appears in the hall. He gently reaches for Wiesel's arm. "Come back," he implores. Wiesel agrees, and the two sit on the sofa. At this point Mauriac begins to weep. He looks at Wiesel but says nothing. Just tears.

Wiesel starts to apologize. Mauriac will have nothing of it. Instead he urges his young friend to talk. He wants to hear about it—the camps, the trains, the deaths. He asks Wiesel why he hasn't put this to paper. Wiesel tells him the pain is too severe. He's made a vow of silence. The older man tells him to break it and speak out.

The evening changed them both. The drama became the soil of a lifelong friendship. They corresponded until Mauriac's death in 1970. "I owe François Mauriac my career," Wiesel has said . . . and it was to Mauriac that Wiesel sent the first manuscript of *Night*.[2]

What if Mauriac had kept the door shut? Would anyone have blamed him? Cut by the sharp words of Wiesel, he could have become impatient with the angry young man and have been glad to be rid of him. But he didn't and he wasn't. He reacted decisively, quickly, and lovingly. He was "slow to boil." And, because he was, a heart began to heal.

May I urge you to do the same?

"God is being patient with you" (2 Pet. 3:9). And if God is being patient with you, can't you pass on some patience to others? Of course you can. Because before love is anything else:

Love is patient.

Your Kindness Quotient

Love is kind.

1 Corinthians 13:4 niv

THE KINDNESS OF JESUS.

WE ARE QUICK TO THINK OF HIS POWER,

HIS PASSION, AND HIS DEVOTION.

BUT THOSE NEAR HIM KNEW AND KNOW

GOD COMES CLOAKED IN KINDNESS.

T hree messages were on my answering machine this morning. All three making the same request. They'd heard the topic of this chapter and wanted to contribute. God had been kind to them. They had a story to share. I invited them over.

The first to arrive was a young couple freshly married. Both showed evidence of a recent wedding—she was thin from the weight she'd lost; he was wide eyed at the bride he'd gained. Sitting cuddly close on the couch, they told me their story. She did most of the talking. He nodded and smiled and would finish a sentence when she stopped for breath.

"My mother and Mary had been friends since they were teens. So we invited Mary and Jesus to the wedding."

"My wife knew Jesus when he ran the family business," he added.

"We were thrilled when Jesus came. But a bit surprised at the vanload of buddies. There was a bunch."

"Fifteen or twenty," he offered.

"But that was fine. After all, Jesus is like family. Besides, we had a great time. Long after the ceremony ended, people lingered. Eating and drinking."

"Drinking a bit too much," the groom explained.

"Yeah, soon the wine was gone, and the waiters were nervous because the people still wanted to party."

The young girl slid to the front of the couch. "I didn't even know about the problem until it was solved. No one told me. Someone told Jesus, though, and he took care of it. Not only did he produce more wine, he improved it!" She went on to say that the wedding coordinator reported that the vintage tasted like the hundred-dollar-a-bottle Bordeaux she tasted once at a wine festival.

The young man moved up to the front of the couch with his wife. "Here is what impresses us." As he spoke, she looked at him and nodded as if she knew what he was going to say. "This is his first miracle, right? His debut, and he uses it on us! To save us from looking like poor hosts."

"He didn't have to do that," she jumped in. "Our town had sick people, poor people. Why, raising the dead would have made the headlines. But he used his premiere miracle on a social miscue. Wasn't that kind of him?" She smiled. He smiled.

So did I.

As they left a businessman came in. Told me his name was Zacchaeus. A short fellow in an Italian suit. All tan and teeth. Cole Haans. Ray·Bans. You could tell he had done well for himself. "Don't let the appearance fool you," he said. "I had the bucks but not the friends. Built this big house on the edge of town. But no one ever came to see me, not even the Jehovah's Witnesses. Can't say I blamed them. I paid for the place with money I'd skimmed off their taxes. No, no one ever visited me till the day Jesus came. 'I'm coming to your house today,' he announced. Right there in the middle of town where all could hear. He didn't have to do that, you know. The diner was down the block, or I would have bought him lunch at the club. But, no, he wanted to come to my house. And he wanted everyone to know where he was going. His is the first signature in my guest book. That was kind of him, don't you think? Unbelievably kind."

Later in the day a woman came by. Middle aged. Hair streaked with gray and pulled back. Dress was simple. Reminded me of a middle-school librarian. Face was wrinkled and earnest. Said she'd been sick for a dozen years. HIV positive.

"That's a long time," I said.

Long enough, she agreed, to run out of doctors, money, even hope. But worst of all, she had run out of friends. "They were afraid of me," she said. "Worried about catching the disease. My church hadn't turned me out, but they hadn't helped me out either. I hadn't been home in years. Been living in a shelter. But then Jesus came to town. He was on his way to treat the mayor's daughter, who was dying. The crowd was thick, and people were pushing, but I was desperate."

She spoke of following Jesus at a distance. Then she drew near and stepped back for fear of being recognized. She told of inching behind a broad-shouldered man and staying in his wake until, as she said, "There were only two people between him and me. I pressed my arm through the mob and reached for the hem of his jacket. Not to grab, just to touch it. And when I did, my body changed. Instantly. My face rushed with warmth. I could breathe deeply. My back seemed to straighten. I stopped, letting the people push past. He stopped too. 'Who touched me?' he asked. I slid behind the big man again and said nothing. As he and the crowd waited, my heart pounded. From the healing? From fear? From both? I didn't know. Then he asked again, 'Who touched me?' He didn't sound angry—just curious. So I spoke up. My voice shook; so did my hands. The big man stepped away. Jesus stepped forward, and I told the whole story."

"The whole story?" I asked.

"The whole story," she replied.

I tried to imagine the moment. Everyone waiting as Jesus listened. The crowd waiting. The city leaders waiting. A girl was dying, people were pressing, disciples were questioning, but Jesus . . . Jesus was listening. Listening to the whole story. He didn't have to. The healing would have been enough. Enough for her. Enough for the crowd. But not enough for him. Jesus wanted to do more than heal her body. He wanted to hear her story—all of it. The whole story. What a kind thing to do. The miracle restored her health. The kindness restored her dignity.

And what he did next, the woman never forgot. "As if he hadn't done enough already"—her eyes began to water—"he called me 'daughter.' 'Daughter, be of good cheer; your faith has made you well. Go in peace.' I've been told he never used that word with anyone else. Just me."[1]

After she left, I checked. She was right.

The kindness of Jesus. We are quick to think of his power, his passion, and his devotion. But those near him knew and know God comes cloaked in kindness. Kind enough to care about a faux pas. Kind enough to have lunch with a crook. Kind enough to bless a suffering sister.

"Love is kind," writes Paul.

Nehemiah agrees: "You are God, ready to pardon, gracious and merciful, slow to anger, abundant in kindness" (Neh. 9:17 NKJV).

David agrees, "Your lovingkindness is better than life" (Ps. 63:3 NASB).

Paul speaks of "the kindness and love of God our Savior" (Titus 3:4 NIV). He is exuberant as he announces: "Now God has us where he wants us, with all the time in this world and the next to shower grace and kindness upon us in Christ Jesus. Saving is all his idea, and all his work. All we do is trust him enough to let him do it" (Eph. 2:7–8 MSG).

But Jesus' invitation offers the sweetest proof of the kindness of heaven:

> Come to Me, all you who labor and are heavy laden, and I will give
> you rest. Take My yoke upon you and learn from Me, for I am gentle
> and lowly in heart, and you will find rest for your souls. For My yoke
> is easy and My burden is light. (Matt. 11:28–30 NKJV)

Farmers in ancient Israel used to train an inexperienced ox by yoking it to an experienced one with a wooden harness. The straps around the older animal were tightly drawn. He carried the load. But the yoke around the younger animal was loose. He walked alongside the more mature ox, but his burden was light. In this verse Jesus is saying, "I walk alongside you. We are yoked together. But I pull the weight and carry the burden."

I wonder, how many burdens is Jesus carrying for us that we know nothing about? We're aware of some. He carries our sin. He carries our shame. He carries our eternal debt. But are there others? Has he lifted fears before we felt them? Has he carried our confusion so we wouldn't have to? Those times when we have been surprised by our own sense of peace? Could it be that Jesus has lifted our anxiety onto his shoulders and placed a yoke of kindness on ours?

And how often do we thank him for his kindness? Not often enough. But does our ingratitude restrict his kindness? No. "Because he is kind even to people who are ungrateful and full of sin" (Luke 6:35).

In the original language, the word for *kindness* carries an added idea the English word does not. Chiefly it refers to an act of grace. But it also refers to a deed or person who is "useful, serviceable, adapted to its purpose."[2] *Kindness* was even employed to describe food that was tasty as well as healthy. Sounds odd to our ears. "Hey, honey, what a great meal. The salad is especially *kind* tonight."

But the usage makes sense. Isn't kindness good *and* good for you? Pleasant *and* practical? Kindness not only says good morning, kindness makes the coffee. Again, doesn't Jesus fit this description? He not only attended the wedding, he rescued it. He not only healed the woman, he honored her. He did more than call Zacchaeus by name; he entered his house.

Hasn't he acted similarly with you? Hasn't he helped you out of a few jams? Hasn't he come into your house? And has there ever been a time when he was too busy to listen to your story? The Bible says, "Whoever is wise will observe these things, and they will understand the lovingkindness of the LORD" (Ps. 107:43 NKJV). Hasn't God been kind—pleasantly useful—to you? And since God has been so kind to you (you know what I am about to say), can't you be kind to others?

Paul's question is for all of us: "Do you think lightly of the riches of His kindness and tolerance and patience, not knowing that the kindness of God leads you to repentance?" (Rom. 2:4 NASB). Repentance from what? Certainly from ungodliness, rebellion, and sin. But can't we equally state that God's kindness leads to repentance from unkindness?

Some may think that all this talk of kindness sounds, well . . . it sounds a bit wimpy. Men in particular tend to value more dramatic virtues—courage, devotion, and visionary leadership. We attend seminars on strategizing and team building. But I can't say I've ever attended or even heard of one lecture on kindness. Jesus, however, would take issue with our priorities. "Go and learn what this means," he commands. "'I want kindness more than I want animal sacrifices'" (Matt. 9:13). Paul places kindness toward the top of the pyramid when he writes, "Love is kind" (1 Cor. 13:4 NIV).

How kind are you? What is your kindness quotient? When was the last time you did something kind for someone in your family—e.g., got a blanket, cleaned off the table, prepared the coffee—without being asked?

Think about your school or workplace. Which person is the most overlooked or avoided? A shy student? A grumpy employee? Maybe he doesn't speak the language. Maybe she doesn't fit in. Are you kind to this person?

Kind hearts are quietly kind. They let the car cut into traffic and the young mom with three kids move up in the checkout line. They pick up the neighbor's trash can that rolled into the street. And they are especially kind at church. They understand that perhaps the neediest person they'll meet all week is the one standing in the foyer or sitting on the row behind them in worship. Paul writes: "When we have the opportunity to help anyone, we should do it. But we should give special attention to those who are in the family of believers" (Gal. 6:10).

And, here is a challenge—what about your enemies? How kind are you to those who want what you want or take what you have?

A friend of mine witnessed a humorous act of kindness at an auction. The purpose of the gathering was to raise money for a school. Someone had donated a purebred puppy that melted the heart and opened the checkbooks of many guests. Two in particular.

They sat on opposite sides of the banquet room, a man and a woman. As the bidding continued, these two surfaced as the most determined. Others dropped off, but not this duo. Back and forth they went until they'd one-upped the bid to several thousand dollars. This was no longer about a puppy. This was about victory. This was the Wimbledon finals, and neither player was backing off the net. (Don't you know the school president was drooling?)

Finally the fellow gave in and didn't return the bid. "Going once, going twice, going three times. Sold!" The place erupted, and the lady was presented with her tail-wagging trophy. Her face softened, then reddened. Maybe she'd forgotten where she was. Never intended to go twelve rounds at a formal dinner. Certainly never intended for the world to see her pit-bull side.

So you know what she did? As the applause subsided, she walked across the room and presented the puppy to the competition.

Suppose you did that with your competition. With your enemy. With the boss who fired you or the wife who left you. Suppose you surprised them with kindness? Not easy? No, it's not. But mercy is the deepest gesture of kindness. Paul equates the two. "Be kind to one another, tenderhearted, forgiving one another, even as God in Christ forgave you" (Eph. 4:32 NKJV). Jesus said:

> Love your enemies. Do good to those who hate you, bless those who curse you. . . . If you love only the people who love you, what praise should you get? . . . [L]ove your enemies, do good to them, and lend to them without hoping to get anything back. Then you will have a great reward, and you will be children of the Most High God, because he is kind even to people who are ungrateful and full of sin. Show mercy, just as your Father shows mercy. (Luke 6:27–28, 32, 35–36)

Kindness at home. Kindness in public. Kindness at church and kindness with your enemies. Pretty well covers the gamut, don't you think? Almost. Someone else needs your kindness. Who could that be? You.

Don't we tend to be tough on ourselves? And rightly so. Like the young couple at the wedding, we don't always plan ahead. Like Zacchaeus, we've cheated our share of friends. We've been self-serving. And like the woman with the illness, our world sometimes seems out of control.

But did Jesus scold the couple? No. Did he punish Zacchaeus? No. Was he hard on the woman? No. He is kind to the forgetful. He is kind to the greedy. He is kind to the sick.

And he is kind to us. And since he is so kind to us, can't we be a little kinder to ourselves? *Oh, but you don't know me, Max. You don't know my faults and my thoughts. You don't know the gripes I grumble and the complaints I mumble.* No, I don't, but he does. He knows everything about you, yet he doesn't hold back his kindness toward you. Has he, knowing all your secrets, retracted one promise or reclaimed one gift?

No, he is kind to you. Why don't you be kind to yourself? He forgives your faults. Why don't you do the same? He thinks tomorrow is worth living. Why don't you agree? He believes in you enough to call you his ambassador, his follower, even his child. Why not take his cue and believe in yourself?

In the book entitled *Sweet Thursday,* John Steinbeck introduces us to Madam Fauna. She runs a brothel and takes a liking to a prostitute by the name of Suzy. Madam Fauna sets Suzy up on a real date with a man, not a client. She buys Suzy a nice dress and helps her get ready for the evening. As Suzy is leaving, she, moved by Madam Fauna's kindness, asks her, "You have done so much for me. Can I do anything for you?"

"Yes," the older woman replies, "you can say, 'I'm Suzy and no one else.'"

Suzy does. Then Madam Fauna requests, "Now say, 'I'm Suzy, and I'm a good thing.'"

And so Suzy tries. "I'm Suzy, and I'm a good . . ." And Suzy begins to cry.

Wouldn't God want you to say the same words? In his book you are a *good thing.* Be kind to yourself. God thinks you're worth his kindness. And he's a good judge of character.

CHAPTER
FOUR

INFLAMED

Love does not envy.
1 CORINTHIANS 13:4 NKJV

GOD OFFERS AUTHENTIC LOVE.

HIS DEVOTION IS THE REAL DEAL.

BUT HE WON'T GIVE YOU THE GENUINE

UNTIL YOU SURRENDER THE IMITATIONS.

Nancy is single. Forty-something and single. Her friends chat about diapers and schools, the oddities of husbands, and the curiosities of family life. She just listens and smiles.

She is single. Forty-something and single. Her friends drive minivans. A high-school classmate has kids bound for college. Nancy drives a compact car and eats most meals alone and feels awkward at baby showers.

She is single. People wonder why. They never say it, but their eyes betray it. "You aren't married?" is the question. *Why not?* is the thought. Is something wrong? Something awry? Abnormal?

Serving on a church staff exacerbates the contrast. She dutifully nods as members tell family holiday stories and husband-wife vacation adventures. She spent last Christmas with her parents, then drove home alone. And she'd enjoy a trip, but travel partners are hard to come by. How can she love the church family when they have what she wants?

She occasionally feels vulnerable at night. What was that noise? She feels self-conscious at parties. *Do I go alone?* And she's having to cope with envy. Not anger. Not red-hot jealousy. Certainly not hatred. Just envy. A flicker of resentment toward women who have what she doesn't. And she's concerned.

Well she should be. For what is a flicker today can turn into a fire tomorrow.

Suppose you spotted a flame in your house. Not a blaze and certainly not a fire, but tiny tongues of heat dancing on the hem of a curtain, on the fringe of the carpet, to the side of the stove. What would you do? How would you react? Would you shrug your shoulders and walk away, saying, "A little fire never hurt any house."

Of course not. You'd put it out. Douse it, stamp it, cover it—anything but allow it. You would not tolerate a maverick flame in your house. Why? Because you know the growth pattern of fire. What is born in innocence is deadly in adolescence. Left untended, fire consumes all that is consumable. You know, for the sake of your house, you don't play with fire.

For the sake of your heart, the same is true. A warning should be offered about the fire in the heart, which, left unchecked, can burst into a hungry flame and consume all that is consumable. The name of the fire? Solomon tagged it. "Jealousy is cruel as the grave. Its flashes are flashes of fire" (Song of Sol. 8:6 RSV).

Paul was equally aggressive in his declaration. "Love does not envy" (1 Cor. 13:4 NKJV). No doubt he'd read about and seen the results of unmanaged jealousy.

Look at Joseph's brothers. They started out taunting and teasing Joseph. Harmless sibling rivalry. But then the flicker became a flame. "His brothers were jealous of him" (Gen. 37:11 NIV). Soon it was easier to dump Joseph into a pit than see him at the dinner table. Before long, Joseph was in Egypt, the brothers were in cahoots, and Jacob, the father, was in the dark. He thought his boy was dead. All because of envy.

And what about the Pharisees? Were they evil men? Criminals? Thugs?

No, they were the pastors and teachers of their day. Little League coaches and carpool partners. But what did they do with Jesus? "They had handed Him over because of envy" (Matt. 27:18 NKJV).

And Max, don't forget Max. As long as we are listing the names of people prone to jealousy, put my name on the list. I began smelling smoke when I learned of a church across town. A friend came back with this report: "The church is great! It's bursting at the seams! It's the largest one in town."

A more spiritual Max would have rejoiced. A more mature Max would have thanked God. But the Max who heard the report didn't act mature or spiritual. He acted jealous. Can you believe it? Rather than celebrate God's work, I was obsessed with my own. I wanted our church to be the biggest.

Sickening. The Lord didn't leave me to indulge in such territorialism for long. In a profound moment of conviction, he let me know that the church is his church, not mine. The work is his work, not mine. And my life is his life, not mine.

My job was not to question him but to trust him. "Don't be jealous. . . . Trust the LORD and do good" (Ps. 37:1, 3). The cure for jealousy? Trust. The cause of jealousy? Distrust. The sons of Jacob didn't trust God to meet their needs. The Pharisees didn't trust God to solve their problems. The writer of this book didn't trust God to expand his kingdom. I didn't do so at great risk. What are the consequences of envy?

Loneliness tops the list. Solomon says, "Anger is cruel and destroys like a flood, but no one can put up with jealousy!" (Prov. 27:4). Who wants to hang out with a jealous fool? In a cemetery in England stands a grave marker with the inscription: SHE DIED FOR WANT OF THINGS. Alongside that marker is another, which reads: HE DIED TRYING TO GIVE THEM TO HER.[1]

Sickness is another consequence. The wise man also wrote, "Peace of mind means a healthy body, but jealousy will rot your bones" (Prov. 14:30).

Violence is the ugliest fruit. "You want something you don't have, and you will do anything to get it. You will even kill!" (James 4:2 CEV). "Jealousy," informs Proverbs 6:34, "enrages a man" (NASB). The Jews used one word for jealousy, *qua-nah*. It meant "to be intensely red." Let me ask you, have you seen such envy? Have you seen red-faced jealousy? Are you acquainted with the crimson forehead and the bulging veins? And—be honest now—have they appeared on your face?

If so, you need to do what Nancy did. Stop listing what you want, and start trusting God to provide what you need. Listen to her story:

> It was a few days before my . . . annual staff Christmas party. It came to my attention that I might be one of the few singles in attendance. It was such a dreadful thought, and of course, I truly didn't want to go! But as I prayed, I realized that God wanted me to go and HE wanted to be my partner. I didn't know how this could happen, but I began to pray that I would recognize His presence beside me every moment and that I would radiate that presence. So, "we" went to the party!
>
> As "we" entered, I immediately saw a potential male interest with a beautiful woman. It didn't faze me. As "we" walked from room to room, I socialized, encouraged those I saw, and truly practiced putting others first. As "we" left that evening and got into my car for the long drive home, I burst into tears . . . tears of joy and pain. I rejoiced to feel the peace and presence of Jesus in a tangible way, despite the pain of singleness.
>
> The following Monday a friend stopped by my office and said, "I noticed you at the party and wondered if it might be hard for you to be there alone. But I just wanted to tell you that you radiated God's joy that night."

Since then, I've attended countless weddings, receptions, class reunions, and parties with Jesus as my partner. I can't say it's been easy, but I know that with each event my faith has grown. Jesus is a real, tangible presence—as real to me as any other person. I continue to grow in my understanding of what it means to partner with Him daily in the small things and the big things and what it means for Him to be the ever-present, always available lover of my soul.[2]

God withholds what we desire in order to give us what we need. You desire a spouse; he gives you himself. You seek a larger church; he prefers a stronger church. You want to be healed so you can serve. He wants you confined so you can pray. Such is the testimony of Joni Eareckson Tada. Three decades after a diving accident rendered her a quadriplegic, she and her husband, Ken, visited Jerusalem. Sitting in her wheelchair, she remembered the story of the paralytic Jesus healed at the pool of Bethesda. Thirty years earlier she'd read the account and asked Jesus to do the same for her.

That day in Jerusalem she thanked God that he had answered a higher prayer. Joni now sees her chair as her prayer bench and her affliction as her blessing. Had he healed her legs, thousands of prayers would have been sacrificed to her busy life. She sees that now. She accepts that now. Jealousy was eclipsed by gratitude as she surrendered her will to his.[3]

Nancy trusted her Father with her singleness.

Joni trusted her Father with her disability.

And Susie trusted her father with her pearls. At the age of six her most treasured possession was a string of pearls. The fact that they were fake didn't bother her. She wore them everywhere and played with them every day. She loved the pearls.

She also loved her daddy. His business often took him away for days at a time. The first day home would always be one of celebration. As an adult

Susie can still remember the time he spent a week in the Orient. When he finally returned, the daddy and daughter played all afternoon. As he put her to bed, he asked this question: "Do you love me?"

"Yes, Daddy. I love you more than anything."

"More than anything?"

"More than anything."

He paused for a moment. "More than the pearls? Would you give me your pearls?"

"Oh, Daddy," she replied. "I couldn't do that. I love my pearls."

"I understand," he told her and kissed her good-night.

As she fell asleep, she thought about his request. When she awoke, she thought about it some more. It was on her mind that morning and later in the day. Finally, that night, she went to him with her pearls. "Daddy, I love you more than these. Here, you take them."

"I'm so glad to hear that," he said, standing and opening his attaché case. "I brought you a gift."

She opened the small flat box and gasped. Pearls. Genuine pearls.[4]

You suppose your Father wants to give you some as well? He offers authentic love. His devotion is the real deal. But he won't give you the genuine until you surrender the imitations.

What pearls is he hoping you'll release? What costume jewelry would he love for you to drop? Would you exchange the lesser gifts for the highest gift of knowing God? If you would, then your envy will pass. Jealousy has no fire when true love is received.

GOD'S "NO PECKING" ZONE

Love . . . does not boast,
it is not proud.
1 CORINTHIANS 13:4 NIV

That's what love does. It puts the beloved before itself.

Your soul was more important than his blood.

Your eternal life was more important than his earthly life.

Your place in heaven was more important to him

than his place in heaven,

so he gave up his so you could have yours.

The temperature is in the twenties. The chill factor is single digit. The West Texas wind stings the ears, and frozen grass cracks beneath the step. It is a cold December day. Even the cattle are smart enough to stay in the barn on a morning like this.

Then what am I doing outside? What am I doing standing in a ditch, ankle deep in water, hunkered over a leaking pipe? And, most of all, why aren't the three guys in the truck helping me? Why are they in there while I'm out here? Why are they warm while I'm cold? Why are they dry while I'm wet?

The answer is found in two words: *pecking order.*

We can thank Norwegian naturalists for the term. They are the ones who studied the barnyard caste system. By counting the number of times chickens give and receive pecks, we can discern a chain of command. The alpha bird does most of the pecking, and the omega bird gets pecked. The rest of the chickens are somewhere in between.

That day in the oil field, our alpha bird was the crew chief. Beneath him was a former foreman and beneath the foreman, an illegal immigrant. I was the omega bird. College students on Christmas break come in last.

Our truck-seating assignments revealed our rank. The crew chief drove; second in command got the window seat. Third in line sat in the middle, and the bottom dweller straddled the stick shift. No one announced the system or wrote it down. We just knew it. And when the time came for someone to climb out of the truck and into the ditch, no one had to tell me. I understood the pecking order.

You do too. You know the system. Pecking orders are a part of life. And, to an extent, they should be. We need to know who is in charge. Ranking systems can clarify our roles. The problem with pecking orders is not the order. The problem is with the pecking.

Just ask the shortest kid in class or the janitor whose name no one knows or cares to know. The minority family can tell you. So can the new fellow on the factory line and the family scapegoat. It's not pleasant to be the plankton in the food chain.

A friend who grew up on a farm told me about a time she saw their chickens attacking a sick newborn. She ran and told her mother what was happening. Her mother explained, "That's what chickens do. When one is really sick, the rest peck it to death."

For that reason God says that love has no place for pecking orders. Jesus won't tolerate such thinking. Such barnyard mentality may fly on the farm but not in his kingdom. Just listen to what he says about the alpha birds of his day:

> They do good things so that other people will see them. They make the boxes of Scriptures that they wear bigger, and they make their special prayer clothes very long. Those Pharisees and teachers of the law love to have the most important seats at feasts and in the synagogues. They love people to greet them with respect in the marketplaces, and they love to have people call them "Teacher." (Matt. 23:5–7)

Jesus blasts the top birds of the church, those who roost at the top of the spiritual ladder and spread their plumes of robes, titles, jewelry, and choice seats. Jesus won't stand for it. It's easy to see why. How can I love others if my eyes are only on me? How can I point to God if I'm pointing at me? And, worse still, how can someone see God if I keep fanning my own tail feathers?

Jesus has no room for pecking orders. Love "does not boast, it is not proud" (1 Cor. 13:4 NIV).

His solution to man-made caste systems? A change of direction. In a world of upward mobility, choose downward servility. Go down, not up. "Regard one another as more important than yourselves" (Phil. 2:3 NASB). That's what Jesus did.

He flip-flopped the pecking order. While others were going up, he was going down.

> Your attitude should be the same as that of Christ Jesus: Who, being in very nature God, did not consider equality with God something to be grasped, but made himself nothing, taking the very nature of a servant, being made in human likeness. And being found in appearance as a man, he humbled himself and became obedient to death—even death on a cross! (Phil. 2:5–8 NIV)

Would you do what Jesus did? He swapped a spotless castle for a grimy stable. He exchanged the worship of angels for the company of killers. He could hold the universe in his palm but gave it up to float in the womb of a maiden.

If you were God, would you sleep on straw, nurse from a breast, and be clothed in a diaper? I wouldn't, but Christ did.

If you knew that only a few would care that you came, would you still come? If you knew that those you loved would laugh in your face, would you still care? If you knew that the tongues you made would mock you, the mouths you made would spit at you, the hands you made would crucify you, would you still make them? Christ did. Would you regard the immobile and invalid more important than yourself? Jesus did.

He humbled himself. He went from commanding angels to sleeping in the straw. From holding stars to clutching Mary's finger. The palm that held the universe took the nail of a soldier.

Why? Because that's what love does. It puts the beloved before itself. Your soul was more important than his blood. Your eternal life was more important than his earthly life. Your place in heaven was more important to him than his place in heaven, so he gave up his so you could have yours.

He loves you that much, and because he loves you, you are of prime importance to him.

Christ stands in contrast to the barnyard. He points to the sparrow, the most inexpensive bird of his day, and says, "Five sparrows are sold for only two pennies, and God does not forget any of them. . . . You are worth much more than many sparrows" (Luke 12:6–7).

God remembers the small birds of the world. We remember the eagles. We make bronze statues of the hawk. We name our athletic teams after the falcons. But God notices the sparrows. He makes time for the children and takes note of the lepers. He offers the woman in adultery a second chance and the thief on the cross a personal invitation. Christ is partial to the beat up and done in and urges us to follow suit. "When you give a feast, invite the poor, the crippled, the lame, and the blind" (Luke 14:13).

Want to love others as God has loved you? Come thirsty. Drink deeply of God's love for you, and ask him to fill your heart with a love worth giving. A love that will enable you to:

Put others before yourself. Esther Kim knows what this means. For thirteen years she had one dream. The Summer Olympics. She wanted to represent the United States on the Olympic tae kwon do squad.

From the age of eight, she spent every available hour in training. In fact, it was in training that she met and made her best friend, Kay Poe. The two worked so hard for so long that no one was surprised when they both qualified for the 2000 Olympic trials in Colorado Springs.

Everyone, however, was surprised when they were placed in the same division. They'd never competed against each other, but when the number of divisions was reduced, they found their names on the same bracket. It would be just a matter of events before they found themselves on the same mat. One would win and one would lose. Only one could go to Australia.

As if the moment needed more drama, two facts put Esther Kim in a heartrending position. First, her friend Kay injured her leg in the match prior to theirs. Kay could scarcely walk, much less compete. Because of the injury Esther could defeat her friend with hardly any effort.

But then there was a second truth. Esther knew that Kay was the better fighter. If she took advantage of her crippled friend, the better athlete would stay home.

So what did she do? Esther stepped onto the floor and bowed to her friend and opponent. Both knew the meaning of the gesture. Esther forfeited her place. She considered the cause more important than the credit.[1]

This is a good time for a few poignant questions. What's more important to you—that the work be done or that you be seen? When a brother or sister is honored, are you joyful or jealous? Do you have the attitude of Jesus? Do you consider others more important than yourself?

May I share the first time I felt the force of that challenge?

Harold suffered from cerebral palsy. The condition left him unable to walk, dress, feed himself, or go to the rest room. My job was to help him with each. And I didn't like it. I had moved to St. Louis for spiritual training.

Fresh out of college and ready to change the world. Ready to preach, ready to travel, ready to make history. But I wasn't ready to help Harold.

The director of our internship program had other plans. One day he told me he had a special assignment. I assumed he meant a promotion. I never thought he meant Harold.

Harold loved Bible classes and worship services. My job was to help him attend both. To pick him up, to clean him up. To wheel him in, sit next to him, and take him home. To hold his fork when he ate, to wipe his mouth when he drooled. I don't remember feeling very loving. I do remember the day we studied Philippians 2:3: "In humility consider others better than yourselves" (NIV).

After the teacher read the passage, he asked this question: "Think about the person to your left. Do you consider him more important than yourself?" I looked to my left. Guess who I saw? Harold. His head had fallen forward, mouth open.

Harold more important than me? I had the health, the glib tongue, the (ahem) hours of graduate work. How could I regard him as more important?

But God convicted me of my arrogance and began to work on my attitude. Slowly, but markedly, I became content to be Harold's caretaker. By the end of the year Harold and I had become fast friends. God worked a quiet, yet indelible, miracle in my heart. When word of Harold's death reached me a year ago, I thanked God for letting me know such a teacher as Harold. God uses people like him to remind us: *Put others before yourself.*

And then:

Accept your part in his plan. God uses people like Bob Russell to illustrate this kind of love. Bob ministers at the Southeast Christian Church in Louisville, Kentucky. When Bob began his service there in 1966, the church had 125 members, and Bob was twenty-two years old. During the last three and a half decades, God has built this church into one of his finest and largest families. Over 16,000 people gather each weekend to worship in one of several services.

In 1989 Bob made a choice that surprised many observers. He announced that he was going to share the preaching duties with a twenty-seven-year-old preacher. He and Dave Stone would begin coministering to the church. In the announced plan, each year Bob would preach less and Dave would preach more, thus providing Bob more time to lead the church and the church an experienced successor.

Not everyone could do that. Larger egos in smaller churches have struggled to surrender the pulpit. But Bob understands the danger of the pecking order and is humble enough to invert it.

True humility is not thinking lowly of yourself but thinking accurately of yourself. The humble heart does not say, "I can't do anything." But rather, "I can't do everything. I know my part and am happy to do it."

When Paul writes "*consider* others better than yourselves" (Phil. 2:3 NIV, emphasis mine), he uses a verb that means "to calculate," "to reckon." The word implies a conscious judgment resting on carefully weighed facts.[2] To consider others better than yourself, then, is not to say you have no place; it is to say that you know your place. "Don't cherish exaggerated ideas of yourself or your importance, but try to have a sane estimate of your capabilities by the light of the faith that God has given to you" (Rom. 12:3 PHILLIPS).

And finally:

Be quick to applaud the success of others. To the Romans, Paul gives this counsel: "Give each other more honor than you want for yourselves" (Rom. 12:10).

William Barclay tells of a respected educator of a century past. He was known not just for his success but the way he handled it. On one occasion as he stepped to a seat on a platform, the public noticed who he was and began to applaud. Shocked, he turned and asked the man behind him to go ahead. He then began to applaud the man, assuming the applause was for him, and he was quite willing to share in it.[3]

The humble heart honors others.

Again, is Jesus not our example? Content to be known as a carpenter. Happy to be mistaken for the gardener. He served his followers by washing their feet. He serves us by doing the same. Each morning he gifts us with beauty. Each Sunday he calls us to his table. Each moment he dwells in our hearts. And does he not speak of the day when he as "the master will dress himself to serve and tell the servants to sit at the table, and he will serve them" (Luke 12:37)?

If Jesus is so willing to honor us, can we not do the same for others? Make people a priority. Accept your part in his plan. Be quick to share the applause. And, most of all, regard others as more important than yourself. Love does. For love "does not boast, it is not proud" (1 Cor. 13:4 NIV).

Someone is piecing this all together. His thoughts are something like this: *If I think you are more important than I am . . . and you think I am more important than you are . . . and he thinks she is more important than he is . . . and she thinks he is more important than she is . . . then in the end everyone feels important but no one acts important.*

H'm. You think that's what God had in mind?

A CALL TO COMMON COURTESY

Love is not rude.

1 CORINTHIANS 13:5

Jesus always knocks before entering.

He doesn't have to. He owns your heart.

If anyone has the right to barge in, Christ does.

But he doesn't.

That gentle tap you hear? It's Christ.

"Behold, I stand at the door and knock" (Rev. 3:20 nasb).

And when you answer,

he awaits your invitation to cross the threshold.

See the passenger at gate 26? The fellow looking at the ticket agent with the basset-hound eyes? That's me. Yeah, I know, you can't see very well. DFW Airport is packed. Pass out antennae and extra sets of legs, and you'd have a human anthill. We're all over each other.

It's Canada's fault. A front from the north blasted the Midwest, freezing O'Hare and blowing a thousand itineraries to the wind, including mine. When the plane finally disgorged us, we raced through the concourse like Wal-Mart shoppers on the day after Thanksgiving. Pity anything or anyone in our paths. How else were we supposed to make our connections? Even with perfect weather I'd barely catch the final flight of the day to San Antonio.

That explains my hangdog look. I'm pouring what little charm I have on the kind but hassled ticket agent. The plane is overbooked, and she holds my future in her hands. What will she give me—a boarding pass or a hotel voucher?

"Are there any seats left?" I'm winking, but she doesn't notice. I'm sliding a twenty in her direction, but she doesn't see it. She just looks at the screen and sighs, "I'm afraid . . ."

Afraid? Afraid of what?!

"Afraid you'll have to spend the night in the men's room."

"Afraid the only seat left is in the last row, between two sumo wrestlers."

"Afraid you're milking this illustration like a dairy cow, and if you don't get to the point of the chapter, I'll route you through Afghanistan."

But she said none of these. Want to know how she completed the sentence? (Here, take a tissue. You'll be moved.)

"I'm afraid there are no more seats in coach. We are going to have to bump you up to first class. Do you mind if we do that?"

"Do you mind if I kiss you?" So I boarded the plane and nestled down in the wide seat with the extra leg room and smiled like a prisoner on early parole. Not only was I going home, I was going home in style. I leaned back my head, closed my eyes, and . . .

"Hey! Hey! Lady!" My eyes opened. Two rows in front of me a fellow was standing. A short fellow. Didn't need to watch his head to stand up straight. Did need to watch his tone, however. He was rude.

"How does a guy get an extra pillow around here? And what about my drink? My wife and I paid extra to fly first-class. I am accustomed to better attention. I want some service!"

It's not like the flight attendants had nothing to do, mind you. There was the simple matter of making sure the doors were closed and the bins were shut so this already-hour-late flight could lift off. You'd think a fellow could wait on his pillow and Scotch. Not this guy. After all, as we all knew, he had paid extra to fly first-class.

Which may explain the difference between his behavior and mine. I'm not always a good example, but that night I was a poster child for courtesy. You weren't hearing me grumble. I wasn't complaining. No demands from the window seat in row four. I was just happy to be on board. Mr. Got-to-Have-It-Now may have paid for his place. Not me. Mine was a free gift.

And it wasn't the first. God gave me one long before the airlines did. Talk about an upgrade! Not just coach to first class. How about sinner to saint, hellbent to heavenbound, confused to clarified, guilty to justified? If anyone has been bumped up, I have. I'm not only heading home, I'm heading home in style. And I didn't pay a cent. Nor have any of God's children.

But do we sometimes act as if we did? Do we sometimes behave like the pillowless *prima donna* in the first row? Think about his request for a moment. Was it unreasonable? No. A pillow is part of the flight package. *What* he requested was understandable. *The way* he requested it, however, was not.

His timing was poor; he could have waited a few moments. His tone was harsh; the flight attendants didn't deserve condescension. His agenda was selfish. He didn't just want a pillow; he wanted to be the center of attention.

The Bible has a four-letter word for such behavior: *rude*. When defining what love is not, Paul put *rudeness* on the list. "It is not rude" (1 Cor. 13:5 NIV).

The Greek word for *rude* means shameful or disgraceful behavior.

An example of rudeness was recently taken before the courts in Minnesota. A man fell out of his canoe and lost his temper. Though the river was lined with vacationing families, he polluted the air with obscenities. Some of those families sued him. He said, "I have my rights."

God calls us to a higher, more noble concern. Not "What are my rights?" but "What is loving?"

Do you have the right to dominate a conversation? Yes, but is it loving to do so?

Do you have the right to pretend you don't hear your wife speaking? I suppose so. But is it loving?

Is it within your rights to bark at the clerk or snap at the kids? Yes. But is it loving to act this way?

Denalyn has a right to park in the center of the garage. Which she used to do quite often. I'd open the garage door and see her car overlapping half her space and half mine. My response was always a good-natured hint. "Denalyn," I'd say as I entered the house, "some car is taking up its half of the garage in the middle."

Maybe I said it more firmly one day. Perhaps my tone wasn't as chipper. I honestly don't know what happened, but she began parking on her side. I overheard my daughter ask her why she had quit parking in the middle. "Is it that big of a deal, Mom?"

"It's not that big to me. But it seems to be big to your dad. And if it matters to him, it matters to me."

Wasn't that courteous? Wasn't that Christlike? Perhaps you've never placed the word *courteous* next to Christ. I hadn't until I wrote this chapter.

But you know how you never notice double-cab red trucks until your friend says he wants one—then you see a dozen of them? I had never thought much about the courtesy of Christ before, but as I began looking, I realized that Jesus makes Emily Post look like Archie Bunker.

He always knocks before entering. He doesn't have to. He owns your heart. If anyone has the right to barge in, Christ does. But he doesn't. That gentle tap you hear? It's Christ. "Behold, I stand at the door and knock" (Rev. 3:20 NASB). And when you answer, he awaits your invitation to cross the threshold.

That's how he treated the two disciples on the Emmaus road. The resurrected Jesus didn't presume on their hospitality. When they entered the house, he didn't follow. Only when they "urged" him to enter, did he do so (Luke 24:29 NIV). Astounding! Only days before, he had died for their sin. Only hours before, he had defeated their death. Every angel in the universe would gladly be his doormat, but Jesus, ever the gentleman, walks with no swagger.

And when he enters, he always brings a gift. Some bring Chianti and daisies. Christ brings "the gift of the Holy Spirit" (Acts 2:38). And, as he stays, he serves. "For even the Son of Man did not come to be served, but to serve" (Mark 10:45 NIV). If you're missing your apron, you'll find it on him. He's serving the guests as they sit (John 13:4–5). He won't eat until he's offered thanks, and he won't leave until the leftovers are put away (Matt. 14:19–20).

He is courteous enough to tell you his name (Exod. 3:15) and to call you by yours (John 10:3). And when you talk, he never interrupts. Ever been to a doctor who is so busy that he prescribes the medicine before he hears your problem? Jesus isn't like that. He could be. He "knows what you need before you ask him" (Matt. 6:8 NIV). He also knows what you've done before you ask him for forgiveness. "Nothing in all creation can hide from him. Everything is naked and exposed before his eyes" (Heb. 4:13 NLT). A God of lesser courtesy would stop you midsentence with reminders of your past foibles. Not Christ. He is not rude. He listens.

He is even on time. Never late. Never early. If you're checking your watch, it's because you're on a different itinerary. "There is a time for everything" (Eccles. 3:1). And Christ stays on schedule.

He even opens doors for you. Paul could preach at Troas because "the Lord had opened a door" (2 Cor. 2:12 NIV). When I asked my dad why men should open doors for women, his answer was one word: "respect." Christ must have abundant respect for you.

He knocks before he enters. He always brings a gift. Food is served. The table is cleared. Thanks are offered. He knows your name and tells you his, and here is one more.

He pulls out the chair for you. "He raised us up with Christ and gave us a seat with him in the heavens" (Eph. 2:6).

My wife has a heart for single moms. She loves to include a widow or divorcée at the table when we go to a restaurant. Through the years I've noticed a common appreciation from them. They love it when I pull out their chair. More than once they have specifically thanked me. One mom in particular comes to mind. "My," she blushed, brushing the sudden moisture from her eye, "it's been a while since anyone did that."

Has it been a while for you as well? People can be so rude. We snatch parking places. We forget names. We interrupt. We fail to show up. Could you use some courtesy? Has it been a while since someone pulled out your chair?

Then let Jesus. Don't hurry through this thought. Receive the courtesy of Christ. He's your groom. Does not the groom cherish the bride? Respect the bride? Honor the bride? Let Christ do what he longs to do.

For as you receive his love, you'll find it easier to give yours. As you reflect on his courtesy to you, you'll be likely to offer the same.

Did you notice the first five letters of the word *courteous* spell *court*? In old England, to be courteous was to act in the way of the court. The family and servants of the king were expected to follow a higher standard.

So are we. Are we not called to represent the King? Then "let your light shine before men, that they may see your good deeds and praise your Father in heaven" (Matt. 5:16 NIV).

Occasionally our staff members wear shirts that bear the name of our church. On one such day a staffer needed a special pan, and she phoned around until she located it in a store across town. She endured a long drive through heavy traffic only to encounter a gruff store clerk, who told her they no longer carried the product. The staff member started to return tacky with tacky but then remembered she was wearing the shirt—and she changed her behavior.

The truth is, we are all wearing a shirt. "All of you who were baptized into Christ have clothed yourselves with Christ" (Gal. 3:27 NIV). We wear Jesus. And those who don't believe in Jesus note what we do. They make decisions about Christ by watching us. When we are kind, they assume Christ is kind. When we are gracious, they assume Christ is gracious. But if we are brash, what will people think about our King? When we are dishonest, what assumption will an observer make about our Master? No wonder Paul says, "Be wise in the way you act with people who are not believers, making the most of every opportunity. When you talk, you should always be kind and pleasant so you will be able to answer everyone in the way you should" (Col. 4:5–6). Courteous conduct honors Christ.

It also honors his children. When you surrender a parking place to someone, you honor him. When you return a borrowed book, you honor the lender. When you make an effort to greet everyone in the room, especially the ones others may have overlooked, you honor God's children.

In his book *Handyman of the Lord,* William Borders tells the story of a black man whose poverty had left him begging for food. Ringing the front doorbell at a Southern mansion, the man was told to go around to the back, where he would be given something to eat. The owner of the mansion met him on the back porch and said, "First we will bless the food. Repeat after me, 'Our Father, who art in heaven . . .'"

The hungry man replied, "Your Father, who art in heaven . . ."

"No," the owner of the house corrected. "*Our* Father who art in heaven . . ."

Still the beggar said, "Your Father who art in heaven . . ."

Frustrated, the giver of the food asked, "Why do you insist on saying 'your Father' when I keep telling you to say 'our Father'?"

The man answered, "If I say 'our Father,' that would make you and me brothers, and I'm afraid the Lord wouldn't like it, you askin' your brother to come to the back porch to get a piece of bread."[1]

Common courtesy honors God and his children. "Do your best to live in peace with everyone" (Rom. 12:18). Just do your best. You can't control their attitude, but you can manage yours.

Besides, just look where you are sitting. You could've been bumped off. Instead, you've been bumped up. So loosen up and enjoy the journey. You are going home in style.

GETTING THE "I" OUT OF YOUR EYE

Love . . . is not self-seeking.
1 CORINTHIANS 13:4–5 NIV

GET YOUR SELF OUT OF YOUR EYE
BY GETTING YOUR EYE OFF YOUR SELF.
QUIT STARING AT THAT LITTLE SELF,
AND FOCUS ON YOUR GREAT SAVIOR.

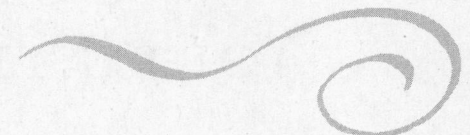

There is a malady that makes the Black Plague appear as mild as the common cold.

Tally the death tolls of all infections, fevers, and epidemics since the beginning of time, and you'll still fall short of the number claimed by this single infirmity.

And, forgive me for being the one to tell you, but you are infected. You suffer from it. You are a victim—a diseased carrier. You have shown the symptoms and manifested the signs. You have a case of—brace yourself—selfishness.

Don't believe me?

Suppose you are in a group photo. The first time you see the picture, where do you look? And if you look good, do you like the picture? If you are the *only* one who looks good, do you still like the picture? If some are cross-eyed and others have spinach in their teeth, do you still like the picture? If that makes you like it even more, you've got a bad case.

What about the physical manifestations?

Clutching hands. Do your fingers ever wrap and close around possessions?

Protruding teeth. Do fangs ever flare when you are interrupted or irritated?

Heavy feet. When a neighboring car wants to cut in front of you, do you sense a sudden heaviness of foot on the accelerator?

Extended shoulder. Any inflammation from patting yourself on the back?

And your neck. Is it sore from keeping your nose in the air?

But most of all, look into your eyes. Look long into your pupils. Do you see a tiny figure? An image of a person? An image of you?

The self-centered see everything through self. Their motto? "It's all about me!" The flight schedule. The traffic. The dress styles. The worship styles. The weather, the work, whether or not one works—everything is filtered through the mini-me in the eye.

Selfishness.

Such a condition can be fatal.

Listen to the words of James. "Whenever people are jealous or selfish, they cause trouble and do all sorts of cruel things" (James 3:16 CEV).

Need proof?

Let's examine one newspaper. Today's edition. How many examples of selfishness will we find in the first few pages?

1. A teenage girl died in a car wreck. Her boyfriend was challenged to a race on a city street. He took the dare and wrapped the car around a telephone pole.
2. The largest petroleum company in the world has filed for bankruptcy. Executives allegedly knew the ship had leaks but told no one until they had time to make huge profits.
3. A prominent citizen is put in jail for child pornography.

Selfishness is to society what the Exxon *Valdez* was to scallops and sea otters—deadly. Is it any wonder that Paul writes: "Do nothing from self-ishness or empty conceit, but with humility of mind regard one another as more important than yourselves; do not *merely* look out for your own personal interests, but also for the interests of others" (Phil. 2:3–4 NASB)?

At first glance the standard in the passage seems impossible to meet. Nothing? We shouldn't do *anything* for ourselves? No new dress or suit. What about going to school or saving money—couldn't all of these things be considered selfish?

They could, unless we are careful to understand what Paul is saying. The word the apostle uses for *selfishness* shares a root form with the words *strife* and *contentious*. It suggests a self-preoccupation that hurts others. A divisive arrogance. In fact, first-century writers used the word to describe a politician who procured office by illegal manipulation or a harlot who seduced the client, demeaning both herself and him.[1] *Selfishness is an obsession with self that excludes others, hurting everyone.*

Looking after your personal interests is proper life management. Doing so to the exclusion of the rest of the world is selfishness. The adverb highlighted in verse 4 is helpful. "Do not *merely* look out for your own personal interests, but also for the interests of others."

Desire success? Fine. Just don't hurt others in achieving it. Wish to look nice? That's okay. Just don't do so by making others look bad. Love isn't selfish.

I was. And I made a mess of things in the process.

A couple of Mondays ago I intended to dedicate the day to sermon preparation. But an urgent call changed everything. *No problem,* I told myself, *I'll start on Tuesday.* Kind people had other ideas. A project had been moved up, and some correspondence needed to be read. Then some bills needed to be paid, and—oh, yes, I forgot about the luncheon. It wasn't the agenda I had in mind. But there was always Wednesday.

On Wednesday the staff meeting went long. I drummed my fingers, but no one took the hint. I cleared my throat and wound my battery-run watch, but no one noticed. Finally the meeting ended, and I could study. "Don't forget to call so-and-so," I was reminded as I left the room. "He's leaving in an hour." *So-and-so* was in a good mood. A chatty mood. I was in a fast mood. A focused mood. Sunday was coming, and the clock was moving. I had the Lord's work to do, and people were in my way.

Finally at midafternoon I sat down. The phone rang. It was my wife. She was in a *disgustingly* good mood. "See you at the ceremony?" she reminded.

"Ceremony?"

"Andrea is graduating from middle school today."

What a dumb day to schedule a graduation ceremony. Everyone knows that diplomas wilt on Wednesdays. "And," she continued, still nauseatingly happy, "could you pick up Jenna from school and bring her home?"

Does this woman not know my calling? Is she unaware of my place in history? Hungry souls need my study. Emaciated minds await my insights. The angels themselves are lining up to grab the front-row Sunday seats— and she wants me to be a chauffeur. "Okay," I growled, not disguising my displeasure.

I was upset. And because I was upset, I chided Jenna for not hurrying to the car.

I was upset. And because I was upset, I forgot to be thankful at the graduation service.

I was upset. And because I was upset, I said, "Let's go, Andrea," instead of saying, "Way to go, Andrea."

I was upset. My day hadn't gone my way. The little Max in my eyes had grown so large I couldn't see anything else.

Apparently God was determined to change all that. At 5:00 P.M. on Wednesday, some fifty-six hours later than I intended to start my preparation, I opened my Bible to read the text of the week and found the very words we've been studying.

> Do nothing from selfishness or empty conceit, but with humility of mind regard one another as more important than yourselves; do not *merely* look out for your own personal interests, but also for the interests of others. (Phil. 2:3–4 NASB)

Remember the passage that describes the Word of God as a sword? I was impaled. As a doctor pronounces a disease, so the passage declared mine. Selfishness. Because of the little me in my eyes, I couldn't see my blessings.

Love builds up relationships; selfishness erodes relationships. No wonder Paul is so urgent in his appeal: "Do nothing from selfishness or empty conceit" (Phil. 2:3 NASB).

But aren't we born selfish? And if so, can we do anything about it? Can we get our eyes off of self? Or, better asked, can we get the little self out of our eyes? According to Scripture, we can.

> Therefore if there is any encouragement in Christ, if there is any consolation of love, if there is any fellowship of the Spirit, if any affection and compassion, make my joy complete by being of the same mind. (Phil. 2:1–2 NASB)

Paul's sarcasm is thinly veiled. Is there any encouragement? Any consolation? Any fellowship? Then smile!

What's the cure for selfishness?

Get your self out of your eye by getting your eye off your self. Quit staring at that little self, and focus on your great Savior.

A friend who is an Episcopalian minister explains the reason he closes his prayers with the sign of the cross. "The touching of my forehead and chest makes a capital 'I.' The gesture of touching first one shoulder, then the other, cuts the 'I' in half."

Isn't that a work of the Cross? A smaller "I" and a greater Christ? Don't focus on yourself; focus on all that you have in Christ. Focus on the encouragement in Christ, the consolation of Christ, the love of Christ, the fellowship of the Spirit, the affection and compassion of heaven.

If Christ becomes our focus, we won't be like the physician in Arkansas. He misdiagnosed the patient. He declared the woman to be dead. The family was informed, and the husband was grief-stricken. Imagine the surprise of the nurse when she discovered that the woman was alive! "You better tell the family," she urged the doctor.

The embarrassed physician phoned the husband and said, "I need to talk to you about the condition of your wife."

"The condition of my wife?" he asked. "She's dead."

The doctor's pride only allowed him to concede, "Well, she has seen a slight improvement."

Slight improvement? Talk about an understatement! Lazarus is walking out of the tomb, and he calls that a "slight improvement"?

He was so concerned about his image that he missed an opportunity to celebrate. We laugh, but don't we do the same? We've gone from cremation to celebration. We deserve a lava bath, but we've been given a pool of grace.

Yet to look at our faces you'd think our circumstances had made only a "slight improvement." "How's life?" someone asks. And we who've been resurrected from the dead say, "Well, things could be better." Or "Couldn't get a parking place." Or "My parents won't let me move to Hawaii." Or "People won't leave me alone so I can finish my sermon on selfishness."

Honestly. We worry about acid rain in silver linings. Do you think Paul might like to have a word with us? Are you so focused on what you don't have that you are blind to what you do? Have you received any encouragement? Any fellowship? Any consolation? Then don't you have reason for joy?

Come. Come thirsty. Drink deeply from God's goodness.

You have a ticket to heaven no thief can take,
an eternal home no divorce can break.

Every sin of your life has been cast to the sea.
Every mistake you've made is nailed to the tree.

You're blood-bought and heaven-made.
A child of God—forever saved.

So be grateful, joyful—for isn't it true?
What you don't have is much less than what you do.

The Headwaters
of Anger

Love . . . is not easily angered.

1 Corinthians 13:4–5 NIV

GOD WILL LOAD YOUR WORLD WITH FLOWERS.

HE HAND-DELIVERS A BOUQUET TO YOUR DOOR EVERY DAY.

OPEN IT! TAKE THEM!

THEN, WHEN REJECTIONS COME, YOU WON'T BE LEFT SHORT-PETALED.

A glance at the two brothers would raise no suspicion. To see them exit the worship service would give you no cause for concern. Like any other set of siblings, they had their differences. One more like Mom, the other more like Dad. One with a bent toward livestock, the other interested in farming. Beyond that, they seemed alike. Compatible. Raised in the same culture. Romped in the same hills. Played with the same animals. Spoke with the same accent. Worshiped the same God.

Then why did one kill the other? Why the violent assault? What made one brother turn on the other and spill his blood? Why did Cain kill Abel?

To answer that question is to shed light on a larger one. Looming behind the question of murder is the question of anger. For "Cain was very angry" (Gen. 4:5 NKJV). Angry indeed. Angry enough to kill. What made him so mad?

Anger in and of itself is not a sin. The emotion was God's idea. "Be angry," he urges, "and do not sin" (Eph. 4:26 NKJV). It's possible to feel what Cain felt without doing what Cain did. Anger is not a sin, but it can lead to sin. Perhaps your anger doesn't lead you to shed blood, but does it make you touchy, irritable, quick-tempered, quick to take offense? Do you fly off the handle? Those aren't my terms. They are Paul's. According to the apostle, love is not:

"touchy" (TLB),

"irritable" (NLT),

"quick tempered" (CEV),

"quick to take offence" (NEB),

"easily angered" (NIV),

and love "doesn't fly off the handle" (MSG).

Cain was all of these and more. But why? Why the short fuse? Again the text gives an answer. "The LORD accepted Abel and his gift, but he did not accept Cain and his gift. So Cain became very *angry* and felt *rejected*" (Gen. 4:4–5, emphasis mine).

Interesting. This is the first appearance of Anger in the Bible. He'll pop up some four hundred more times between here and the maps in the back, but this is the first occasion. He pulls up to the curb and gets out of the car, and look who is in the front seat with him—Rejection. Anger and Rejection in the same sentence.

This isn't the only time the couple are spotted in Scripture. Anger singes many pages. And more than once Rejection is charged with arson.

The sons of Jacob were rejected by their father. He pampered Joseph and neglected them. The result? The brothers were angry. Joseph's "brothers saw that their father loved him more than all his brothers; and so they hated him and could not speak to him on friendly terms" (Gen. 37:4 NASB).

Saul was rejected by his people. In choosing heroes, they chose the fair-haired David over the appointed king. The result? Saul was ticked off. "The women sang as they played, and said, 'Saul has slain his thousands, and David his ten thousands.' Then Saul became very angry" (1 Sam. 18:7–8 NASB).

David's work was rejected by God. His plan to move the ark of the covenant by cart didn't please the Father. And when Uzzah touched what he shouldn't have touched, "God smote him . . . and he died" (2 Sam. 6:7 RSV). Before David was afraid, he fumed. "David became angry because of the LORD's outburst against Uzzah" (2 Sam. 6:8 NASB).

And Jonah. The fellow had a whale of a problem with anger. (Sorry, couldn't resist.) He didn't feel the Ninevites were worthy of mercy, but God did. By forgiving them, God rejected Jonah's opinion. And how did the rejection make Jonah feel? "It greatly displeased Jonah and he became angry" (Jon. 4:1 NASB).

I don't want to oversimplify a complex emotion. Anger has many causes: impatience, unmet expectations, stress, referees who couldn't see a pass-interference call if you painted it on their garage door—oops, sorry, a flashback to a high-school football game. The fire of anger has many logs, but according to biblical accounts, the thickest and the hottest block of wood is rejection.

An odd encounter allowed me to experience this formula firsthand. I was tagging along with my wife and daughters as they went shopping. Such is the life of a father of three girls. Not being an avid shopper myself, I tend to pass the time with a book. We enter a store, they look for sales, I look for chairs. (Hint to retailers: A few recliners would lead to greater sales volume.) This particular store didn't have a chair, however. It was a high-priced, uppity purse store that assumed you'd never want to sit in the presence of their creations. So I found a corner, sat on the floor, and entered the world of fiction.

"Ahem."

Lifting my eyes, I saw pointy-toed high-heeled shoes.

"Ahem, ahem."

Looking up, I saw a female employee with bunned-up hair and black thick-framed glasses.

"Don't sit on the floor," she said.

I thought she was feeling sorry for me. "I don't mind. Besides, I couldn't find a chair."

Her response had the tone of a miffed third-grade teacher. "You aren't *allowed* to sit on the floor."

Not allowed to sit on the floor? Isn't that like saying, "You're not allowed to have your wisdom teeth pulled"? If I'd had another choice, I'd have taken it. "I couldn't find a chair," I told her.

"We don't have chairs," she told me, lowering the room temperature with her frost.

"But I just want to sit down," I replied, my throat starting to tighten.

"We don't want people to sit down," she commanded.

My math was off. This didn't add up. I enter the store with four women who have a weakness for puny purses with foreign names. Shouldn't I be offered a soda and a massage? "I'll stand, all right. I'll stand outside." O-o-o-h, Max, the tough guy.

I leaned against the building and fumed.

Now, why was I angry? What stirred my frustration? In the great scheme of things, the event wouldn't bump a seismic needle. So what bothered me? I narrowed it down to one word. *Rejection.* The salesperson had rejected me. She didn't accept me.

Multiply that emotion by a zillion to understand the anger of an abandoned teen or a divorced spouse. I didn't even know the lady, and I was angry. What happens when you feel the same from your boss, friend, or teacher?

You hurt. And because you get hurt, you get hot. Tacky-toned, cold-shouldered, name-calling, door-slamming, get-my-pound-of-flesh sort of hot. Anger is your defense mechanism.

Envision a teenager receiving a lecture. His dad is going down the list:

poor grades, missed curfews, messy room. Each accusation is like a shove in the boy's chest. Back and back and back until he perceives a Grand Canyon between his father and him. His initial response is silence and shame. Lower and lower he bows. But somewhere a line is crossed, and an innate survival technique kicks in, and he lashes back, "I've had it!" And he stands and storms out.

What about the Hispanic immigrant in the small Anglo town? How many times can a man be teased about his accent, mocked because of his name, and overlooked because of his skin color before he takes a swing at someone?

Consider the wife of the insensitive husband. Every other woman in her office received a card or flowers for Valentine's Day. She kept thinking a delivery boy would stop at her desk, but none ever did. She drives home thinking, *Surely there will be something on the table.* The table is empty. The phone rings. It's him. He'll be late for dinner. No word about Valentine's Day. He forgot. How could he forget? When this happened last year, she was sad. When he did something similar at Christmas, she was hurt. But when he forgot their anniversary, she started to harden. And now this? Her tears are hot. Rejection leads to anger.

And if rejection from people makes us angry, what about when we feel rejected by God? Case study #1? Cain.

The account is sketchy and not without gaps, but we are told enough to re-create the crime scene. Cain and Abel went to worship, perhaps at the same time. They each brought an offering. How did they know to do so? God had told them. Hebrews 11:4 says, "It was by faith that Abel offered God a better sacrifice than Cain did." From where does one get faith? "Faith comes by hearing" (Rom. 10:17 NKJV). Cain and Abel had heard God's instructions. And when Abel brought the best parts of a firstborn from his flock, he did so out of obedience to what he had heard.

And when Cain brought "some food" from the ground, he was acting out of disobedience. Surely he had heard what Abel had heard. Would God hold him accountable otherwise? He knew what Abel knew. He knew that forgiveness of sin came through the shedding of blood (Heb. 9:22). But still he was angry that God returned his sacrifice unopened. God cautioned him to be careful.

God asked Cain, "Why are you angry? Why do you look so unhappy? If you do things well, I will accept you, but if you do not do them well, sin is ready to attack you. Sin wants you, but you must rule over it." At this point in the story, Cain had not sinned. A dose of humility and he would have been fine. But Cain had other plans.

"Cain said to his brother Abel, 'Let's go out into the field.' While they were out in the field, Cain attacked his brother Abel and killed him" (Gen. 4:3–8).

Cain gave up. He gave up on God. He gave up on his ability to please him. And he took it out on Abel. Cain would have related to the frustration of the struggling missionary who wrote:

> God's demands of me were so high, and His opinion of me was so low, there was no way for me to live except under His frown. . . . All day long He nagged me: "Why don't you pray more? Why don't you witness more? When will you ever learn self-discipline? How can you allow yourself to indulge in such wicked thoughts? Do this. Don't do that." . . . When I came down to it, there was scarcely a word or a feeling or a thought or a decision of mine that God really liked.[1]

Many have written letters like that. If not with pen and paper, at least with thoughts. Cain would have penned: "I can't satisfy him. I work in the field and bring my crops. I give him my best, and it's not enough."

Others would write:

"Why won't God hear our prayers! We go to church, we pay our bills, but still the crib is empty."

"Why won't God give me a job? I've done nothing wrong. People who curse him have jobs. I've served him all these years and can't even get an interview."

"What do I have to do to be forgiven? Do I have to spend the rest of my life paying for one mistake?"

Such thoughts will heat your collar. Stoke your anger. Make you snap at those shallow minds like Abel who do half the work but get all the blessings—

Stop for a second. Did you just make a discovery? Did a light go on? Have you for the first time found the headwaters of your anger? Can your bitterness be traced upstream to a feeling of divine rejection? If so (I'm glad to tell you this), in finding the cause you have also found the cure.

When I really want a person to listen to me, I scoot my chair a couple of inches in their direction and lower my voice. If you and I were having a chat about your anger, this is where I'd start scooting, and I'd say the next sentence so softly you'd have to lean forward to hear. So incline a tad and listen to this thought.

If rejection causes anger, wouldn't acceptance cure it? If rejection by heaven makes you mad at others, wouldn't acceptance from heaven stir your love for them? This is the 7:47 Principle. Remember the verse? "He who is forgiven little loves little." We can replace the word *forgiven* with *accepted* and maintain the integrity of the passage. "He who is *accepted* little loves little." If we think God is harsh and unfair, guess how we'll treat people. Harshly and unfairly. But if we discover that God has doused us with unconditional love, would that make a difference?

The apostle Paul would say so! Talk about a turnaround. He went from bully to teddy bear. Paul B.C. (Before Christ) sizzled with anger. He "made havoc of the church" (Acts 8:3 NKJV). Paul A.D. (After Discovery) brimmed with love. Could a raving maniac write these words?

To the Corinthians: "I always thank my God for you" (1 Cor. 1:4).

To the Philippians: "I have you in my heart. . . . I long for all of you with the affection of Christ Jesus" (Phil. 1:7–8 NIV).

To the Ephesians: "I have not stopped giving thanks for you, remembering you in my prayers" (Eph. 1:16 NIV).

To the Colossians: "We always thank God, the Father of our Lord Jesus Christ, when we pray for you" (Col. 1:3 NIV).

To the Thessalonians: "We were gentle among you, like a mother caring for her little children" (1 Thess. 2:7 NIV).

His heart was a universe of love. But what about his enemies? It's one thing to love your coworkers, but did Paul love those who challenged him? "I would be willing to be forever cursed—cut off from Christ!—if that would save them" (Rom. 9:1–3 NLT). On every occasion that he had to enter their synagogues and teach, he did so (Acts 13:4–5; 14:1; 17:1–2, 10). His accusers beat him, stoned him, jailed him, mocked him. But can you find one occasion where he responded in kind? One temper tantrum? One angry outburst? *This is a different man.* His anger is gone. His passion is strong. His devotion is unquestioned. But rash outbursts of anger? A thing of the past.

What made the difference? He encountered Christ. Or, to use his phrase, he was hidden in Christ: "Your life is now hidden with Christ in God" (Col. 3:3 NIV).

The Chinese language has a great symbol for this truth. The word for *righteousness* is a combination of two pictures. On the top is a lamb. Beneath the lamb is a person. The lamb covers the person.[2] Isn't that the essence of righteousness? The Lamb of Christ over the child of God? Whenever the Father looks down on you, what does he see? He sees his

Son, the perfect Lamb of God, hiding you. Christians are like their ancestor Abel. We come to God by virtue of the flock. Cain came with the work of his own hands. God turned him away. Abel came, and we come, dependent upon the sacrifice of the Lamb, and we are accepted. Like the Chinese symbol, we are covered by the lamb, hidden in Christ.

When God looks at you, he doesn't see you; he sees Jesus. And how does he respond when he sees Jesus? He rends the heavens and vibrates the earth with the shout, "You are my Son, whom I love, and I am very pleased with you" (Mark 1:11).

The missionary was wrong. We don't live under the frown of God. We stir an ear-to-ear smile of joy. "He will rejoice over you with gladness, He will quiet you with His love, He will rejoice over you with singing" (Zeph. 3:17 NKJV).

Through Christ, God has accepted you. Think about what this means. I'm scooting forward and talking softly again: *You cannot keep people from rejecting you. But you can keep rejections from enraging you.*

Rejections are like speed bumps on the road. They come with the journey. Tacky purse peddlers populate the world. You're going to get cut, dished, dropped, and kicked around. You cannot keep people from rejecting you. But you can keep rejections from enraging you. How? By letting his acceptance compensate for their rejection.

Think of it this way. Suppose you dwell in a high-rise apartment. On the window sill of your room is a solitary daisy. This morning you picked the daisy and pinned it on your lapel. Since you have only one plant, this is a big event and a special daisy.

But as soon as you're out the door, people start picking petals off your daisy. Someone snags your subway seat. Petal picked. You're blamed for the bad report of a coworker. Three petals. The promotion is given to someone with less experience but USC water polo looks. More petals. By the end of the day, you're down to one. Woe be to the soul who dares to draw near it. You're only one petal-snatching away from a blowup.

What if the scenario was altered slightly? Let's add one character. The kind man in the apartment next door runs a flower shop on the corner. Every night on the way home he stops at your place with a fresh, undeserved, yet irresistible bouquet. These are not leftover flowers. They are top-of-the-line arrangements. You don't know why he thinks so highly of you, but you aren't complaining. Because of him, your apartment has a sweet fragrance, and your step has a happy bounce. Let someone mess with your flower, and you've got a basketful to replace it!

The difference is huge. And the interpretation is obvious.

God will load your world with flowers. He hand-delivers a bouquet to your door every day. Open it! Take them! Then, when rejections come, you won't be left short-petaled.

God can help you get rid of your anger. He made galaxies no one has ever seen and dug canyons we have yet to find. "The LORD . . . heals all your diseases" (Ps. 103:2–3 NIV). Do you think among those diseases might be the affliction of anger?

Do you think God could heal your angry heart?

Do you want him to? This is not a trick question. He asks the same question of you that he asked of the invalid: "Do you want to be well?" (John 5:6). Not everyone does. You may be addicted to anger. You may be a rage junkie. Anger may be part of your identity. But if you want him to, he can change your identity. Do you want him to do so?

Do you have a better option? Like moving to a rejection-free zone? If so, enjoy your life on your desert island.

Take the flowers. Receive from him so you can love or at least put up with others.

Do what T. D. Terry did. Many years ago a stressful job stirred within him daily bouts of anger. His daughter, upon hearing him describe them years later, responded with surprise. "I don't remember any anger during those years."

He asked if she remembered the tree—the one near the driveway about halfway between the gate and the house. "Remember how it used to be tall? Then lost a few limbs? And after some time was nothing more than a stump?"

She did.

"That was me," T. D. explained. "I took my anger out on the tree. I kicked it. I took an ax to it. I tore the limbs. I didn't want to come home mad, so I left my anger at the tree."[3]

Let's do the same. In fact, let's go a step farther. Rather than take out our anger on a tree in the yard, let's take our anger to the tree on the hill. Leave your anger at the tree of Calvary. When others reject you, let God accept you. He is not frowning. He is not mad. He sings over you. Take a long drink from his limitless love, and cool down.

THE HEART FULL
OF HURTS

Love . . . keeps no record of wrongs.

1 CORINTHIANS 13:4–5 NIV

Today's thoughts are tomorrow's actions.

Today's jealousy is tomorrow's temper tantrum.

Today's bigotry is tomorrow's hate crime.

Today's anger is tomorrow's abuse.

Today's lust is tomorrow's adultery.

Today's greed is tomorrow's embezzlement.

Today's guilt is tomorrow's fear.

The *Pelicano* is the world's most unwanted ship. Since 1986 she has been the hobo of the high seas. No one wants her. Sri Lanka doesn't. Bermuda doesn't. The Dominican Republic turned her away. So did the Netherlands, the Antilles, and Honduras.

The problem is not the boat. Though rusty and barnacled, the 466-foot freighter is seaworthy.

The problem is not the ownership. The owners have kept the license current and taxes paid.

The problem is not the crew. They may feel unwanted, but they aren't inefficient.

Then what is the problem? What is the reason for years of rejections? Waved away in Sri Lanka. Turned away in Indonesia. Rejected in Haiti. Why is the *Pelicano* the most unwanted ship in the world?

Simple. She is full of trash. Fifteen thousand tons of trash. Orange peelings. Beer bottles. Newspapers. Half-eaten hot dogs. Trash. The trash of Philadelphia's long summer of 1986. That's when the municipal workers went on strike. That's when the trash piled higher and higher. That's when

Georgia refused it and New Jersey declined it. No one wanted Philadelphia's trash.

That's when the *Pelicano* entered the picture. The owners thought they would turn a quick penny by transporting the rubbish. The trash was burned, and the ashes were dumped into the belly of the boat. But no one would take it. Initially it was too much. Eventually it was too old. Who wants potentially toxic trash?[1]

The plight of the *Pelicano* is proof. Trash-filled ships find few friends. The plight of the *Pelicano* is also a parable. Trash-filled hearts don't fare any better.

I wonder if you can relate to the *Pelicano*. Are you unwanted at the dock? Drifting farther from friends and family? If so, you might check your heart for garbage. Who wants to offer dock space to a smelly heart?

Life has a way of unloading her rubbish on our decks. Your husband works too much. Your wife gripes too much. Your boss expects too much. Your kids whine too much. The result? Trash. Load after load of anger. Guilt. Pessimism. Bitterness. Bigotry. Anxiety. Deceit. Impatience. It all piles up.

Trash affects us. It contaminates our relationships. It did Cain's. He had anger in his mind before he had blood on his hands. And Martha? Martha was meddlesome in her attitude before she was quarrelsome with her tongue. And what about the Pharisees? They killed Christ in their hearts before they killed him on the cross.

Mark it down. Today's thoughts are tomorrow's actions.

Today's jealousy is tomorrow's temper tantrum.

Today's bigotry is tomorrow's hate crime.

Today's anger is tomorrow's abuse.

Today's lust is tomorrow's adultery.

Today's greed is tomorrow's embezzlement.

Today's guilt is tomorrow's fear.

Today's thoughts are tomorrow's actions. Could that be why Paul writes, "Love . . . keeps no record of wrongs" (1 Cor. 13:5 NIV)? Let trash on board, and people are going to smell it. The troubles for the *Pelicano* began with the first shovelful. The crew should have turned it away at the gate. Life would have been easier for everyone on board if they had never allowed the trash to pile up.

Life will be better for you if you do the same.

Some folks don't know we have an option. To listen to our vocabulary you'd think we are the victims of our thoughts. "Don't talk to me," we say. "I'm in a bad mood." As if a mood were a place to which we were assigned ("I can't call you. I'm in Bosnia.") rather than an emotion we permit.

Or we say, "Don't mess with her. She has a bad disposition." Is a disposition something we "have"? Like a cold or the flu? Are we the victims of the emotional bacteria of the season? Or do we have a choice?

Paul says we do: "We capture every thought and make it give up and obey Christ" (2 Cor. 10:5).

Do you hear some battlefield jargon in that passage—"capture every thought," "make it give up" and "obey Christ"? You get the impression that we are the soldiers and the thoughts are the enemies. Our assignment is to protect the boat and refuse entrance to trashy thoughts. The minute they appear on the dock we go into action. "This heart belongs to God," we declare, "and you aren't getting on board until you change your allegiance."

Selfishness, step back! Envy, get lost! Find another boat, Anger! You aren't allowed on this ship. Capturing thoughts is serious business.

It was for Jesus. Remember the thoughts that came his way courtesy of the mouth of Peter? Jesus had just prophesied his death, burial, and resurrection, but Peter couldn't bear the thought of it. "Peter took Jesus aside and told him not to talk like that. . . . Jesus said to Peter, 'Go away from me, Satan! You are not helping me! You don't care about the things of God, but only about the things people think are important'" (Matt. 16:22–23).

See the decisiveness of Jesus? A trashy thought comes his way. He is tempted to entertain it. A cross-less life would be nice. But what does he do? He stands at the gangplank of the dock and says, "Get away from me." As if to say, "You are not allowed to enter my mind."

What if you did that? What if you took every thought captive? What if you refused to let any trash enter your mind? What if you took the counsel of Solomon: "Be careful what you think, because your thoughts run your life" (Prov. 4:23).

You are driving to work when the words of your coworker come to mind. He needled you about your performance. He second-guessed your efficiency. Why was he so hard on you? You begin to wonder. *I didn't deserve any of that. Who is he to criticize me? Besides, he has as much taste as a rice cake. Have you seen those shoes he wears?*

At this point you need to make a choice. *Am I going to keep a list of these wrongs?* You can. Standing on the gangplank is Self-pity and her seven sisters. They want on board. Are you going to let them? If you do, you'll be as smelly as the *Pelicano* by the time you reach your office.

Or you can do something else. You can take those thoughts captive. You can defy the culprit. Quote a verse if you have to: "Bless those who persecute you; bless and do not curse" (Rom. 12:14 NIV).

Another scene. Anger at your parents is keeping you awake. You want to sleep, but this afternoon's phone call won't let you. As always, all they did was criticize. No compliments. No applause. Just pick, pick, pick. Why aren't you married? When are you coming home? Why don't you have a good job like your cousin Homer at the bank? Grrrr. See that fellow at the bottom of the gangplank? The one wearing the dark robe? He's a judge from the court of critical attitudes. Judge Mental. Let him on board, and the two of you can spend the night passing out guilty verdicts. You can alphabetize and codify all the parents' mistakes. Are you going to let him on board? Do so at great risk, my friend. By morning you'll be smelling like a landfill.

Remember, just because there is trash on the dock, that doesn't mean there must be trash on your ship. You are not a victim of your thoughts. You have a vote. You have a voice. You can exercise thought prevention. You can also exercise thought permission.

How could you change the plight of the *Pelicano*? Change her cargo. Load the decks with flowers instead of trash, presents instead of ash, and no one would turn the ship away. Change the cargo, and you change the ship.

By the same token, change the thoughts, and you change the person. If today's thoughts are tomorrow's actions, what happens when we fill our minds with thoughts of God's love? Will standing beneath the downpour of his grace change the way we feel about others?

Paul says absolutely! It's not enough to keep the bad stuff out. We've got to let the good stuff in. It's not enough to keep no list of wrongs. We have to cultivate a list of blessings. The same verb Paul uses for *keeps* in the phrase "keeps no list of wrongs" is used for *think* in Philippians 4:8: "Whatever is true, whatever is honorable, whatever is just, whatever is pure, whatever is lovely, whatever is gracious, if there is any excellence, if there is anything worthy of praise, think about these things" (RSV). *Thinking* conveys the idea of pondering—studying and focusing, allowing what is viewed to have an impact on us.

Rather than store up the sour, store up the sweet.

You want to make a list? Then list his mercies. List the times God has forgiven you. Stand face to feet with the form of your crucified Savior and pray, "Jesus, if you can forgive me for hurting you, then I can forgive them for hurting me." You didn't deserve to be hurt by them. But neither did you deserve to be forgiven by him.

But, Max, I'm a decent person. I've never done anything to hurt Christ. Be careful now. That opinion can lead to trouble. Do you really think you haven't done things that hurt Christ?

Have you ever been dishonest with his money? That's cheating.

Has your love for flesh or fame ever turned you away from him? That's adultery.

Ever spoken an angry word with the intent to hurt? In the corpus juris of heaven, you are guilty of assault.

Have you ever been silent while he was mocked? Don't we call that treason?

Ever gone to church to be seen rather than to see him? Hypocrite.

Ever broken a promise you've made to God? Whoa. Deceit. That's serious.

Need we go further? Only six questions, just two inches of copy, and look at you. Guilty of dishonesty, adultery, assault, treason, hypocrisy, and deceit. A list worthy of indictment. Don't you deserve to be punished? And yet, here you are. Reading this book. Breathing. Still witnessing sunsets and hearing babies gurgle. Still watching the seasons change. There are no lashes on your back or hooks in your nose or shackles on your feet. Apparently God hasn't kept a list of your wrongs. Apparently David knew what he was saying: "[God] has not punished us as our sins should be punished; he has not repaid us for the evil we have done" (Ps. 103:10). And he meant it when he prayed, "LORD, if you kept a record of our sins, who, O Lord, could ever survive?" (Ps. 130:3 NLT).

Listen. You have not been sprinkled with forgiveness. You have not been spattered with grace. You have not been dusted with kindness. You have been immersed in it. You are submerged in mercy. You are a minnow in the ocean of his mercy. Let it change you! See if God's love doesn't do for you what it did for the woman in Samaria.

Talk about a woman who could make a list. Number one, discrimination. She is a Samaritan, hated by Jews. Number two, gender bias. She is a female, condescended to by the men. Third, she is a divorcée, not once, not twice. Let's see if we can count. Four? Five? Five marriages turned south, and now she's sharing a bed with a guy who won't give her a ring.

When I add this up, I envision a happy-hour stool sitter who lives with her mad at half boil. Husky voice, cigarette breath, and a dress cut low at the top and high at the bottom. Certainly not Samaria's finest. Certainly not the woman you'd put in charge of the Ladies' Bible class.

Which makes the fact that Jesus does just that all the more surprising. He doesn't just put her in charge of the class; he puts her in charge of evangelizing the whole town. Before the day is over, the entire city hears about a man who claims to be God. "He told me everything I ever did" (John 4:39), she tells them, leaving unsaid the obvious, "and he loved me anyway."

A little rain can straighten a flower stem. A little love can change a life. Who knew the last time this woman had been entrusted with anything, much less the biggest news in history! In fact, flip to the left out of John 4, and you'll make this startling discovery. She is Jesus' missionary! She precedes the more noted. The lineage of Peter and Paul, St. Patrick and St. Francis of Assisi can be traced back to a town trollop who was so overwhelmed by Christ that she had to speak.

Another *Pelicano* forever fumigated. Why?

Not just because of what Jesus did, though that was huge. But because she let him do it. She let him on board. She let him love her. She let him change her cargo. He found her full of trash and left her full of grace. She and Zacchaeus and the apostle Paul and the woman in Capernaum and millions of others invited him into the hold of their hearts.

She didn't have to.

They didn't have to.

And you don't have to.

You really don't.

You can stick with your long lists and stinky cargo. And drift from port to port.

But why would you? Let the *Pelicano* have the high seas.

Your Captain has better plans for you.

CHAPTER
TEN

THE LOVE TEST

*Love does not delight in evil
but rejoices with the truth.*

1 CORINTHIANS 13:6 NIV

Isn't it good to know that even when we don't love with a perfect love, he does?

A jog wasn't on my mind when we checked into the hotel. It was dark. Waco, Texas, was windy and cold. The book tour was fun but tiring—third city in three days. I was just happy to get to bed. A good night's rest changed things, however. So did the bright sun and warm morning. I laced up my shoes, waved good-bye to the desk clerk, and took off through the neighborhood.

Running through unfamiliar towns can be tricky. I once spent three hours seeing parts of Fresno that most citizens of Fresno have never seen. So, to keep my bearings, I stay on one road. Run out. Run back.

The run back to the hotel seemed longer, but I chalked it up to poor conditioning. Upon entering the lobby, I noticed a breakfast buffet. One of those free ones where you toast your own toast and heat your own oatmeal. *Fine by me,* I thought, wondering why I hadn't noticed the food when I left.

I filled a tray, ate the meal, and was going back for seconds when I heard a couple of Brazilians speaking. For five years Brazil was home to our family. I couldn't resist a good conversation. *"Bom dia,"* I greeted. We talked about the country, the economy. I shared the only Portuguese joke I remembered. They invited me to take a seat. "Let me refill my coffee cup first," I replied. I returned and took a seat, not just with coffee, but more toast.

As I left to clean up, I passed the food bar again and, believe it or not, was still hungry. *No harm,* I reasoned. Calculating in the jog, I figured I'd break even. So I filled a bowl with oatmeal and decided to eat it in my room.

I walked straight through the lobby, turned right at the first hallway, past the indoor pool (h'm, I didn't notice a pool last night), and came to the first door on the right. But something was wrong. My key card wouldn't open the door. Tried a second time. No luck. I looked up at the room number. *Wait a minute, this isn't my room!*

I retraced my steps. Back down the hall. Past the pool. (How could I not notice that pool?) Back into the lobby. Past the breakfast bar. Smile at the manager. Surely she wonders where I'm headed with the food. Out the front door. Into the parking lot. I looked up at the sign over the entrance. *This isn't my hotel! Where is my hotel?* I looked to the right. Then to the left. There it was! Next door. Well, what do you know? I'd jogged past my place and into this one. Duh! What else to do but shrug and walk across the lot and to my room? (I took the oatmeal with me. They wouldn't have wanted it back.)

I'd spent an hour in the wrong hotel. Visiting in the lobby. Chatting with the guests. Eating the food. Drinking the coffee. I even complimented the manager on the decorations. For an hour I was in the wrong hotel. And you know what?

I *felt* as though I was in the right place. Had you asked me what I was doing eating a free meal in the wrong hotel, I would have looked at you as if you were wearing hockey clothes in the Amazon. "You're crazy."

Not once did I lift my head and furrow my brow and think, *This place feels funny.* It didn't. It *felt* fine. But my feelings were wrong. My key card proved them wrong. The room number proved them wrong. The manager, had she been asked, could have proved them wrong. No matter how much I felt as though I was in the right place, I was not. And no mountain of feelings could change that.

I wonder if you've ever made the same mistake. Not with a hotel, but with love. Have you ever made decisions about your relationships based on your feelings instead of the facts? When it comes to love, feelings rule the day. Emotions guide the ship. Goose bumps call the shots. But should they? Can feelings be trusted? Can a relationship feel right but be wrong? Heads are nodding.

A single mom is nodding.

A college kid with a broken heart is nodding.

The fellow who fell in love with a figure that could cause a twelve-car pileup is nodding.

Feelings can fool you. Yesterday I spoke with a teenage girl who is puzzled by the lack of feelings she has for a guy. Before they started dating, she was wild about him. The minute he showed interest in her, however, she lost interest.

I'm thinking also of a young mom. Being a parent isn't as romantic as she anticipated. Diapers and midnight feedings aren't any fun, and she's feeling guilty because they aren't. *Am I low on love?* she wonders.

How do you answer such questions? Ever wish you had a way to assess the quality of your affection? A DNA test for love? Paul offers us one: "Love does not delight in evil but rejoices with the truth" (1 Cor. 13:6 NIV). In this verse lies a test for love.

Want to separate the fake from the factual, the counterfeit from the real thing? Want to know if what you feel is genuine love? Ask yourself this:

Do I encourage this person to do what is right? For true love "takes no pleasure in other people's sins but delights in the truth" (1 Cor. 13:6 JB).

For instance, one lady calls another and says, "We're friends, right?"

"Yeah, we're friends."

"If my husband asks, you tell him we were together at the movies last night."

"But we weren't."

"I know, but I was, well, I was with another guy and—hey, you'll do this for me, won't you? We're friends, right? Tighter than sisters, right?"

Does this person pass the test? No way. The room key doesn't work. Love doesn't ask someone to do what is wrong. How do we know? "Love does not delight in evil but rejoices with the truth" (1 Cor. 13:6 NIV).

If you find yourself prompting evil in others, heed the alarm. This is not love. And if others prompt evil in you, be alert. Check the room key.

Here's an example. A classic one. A young couple are on a date. His affection goes beyond her comfort zone. She resists. But he tries to persuade her with the oldest line in the book: "But I love you. I just want to be near you. If you loved me . . ."

That siren you hear? It's the phony-love detector. This guy doesn't love her. He may love having sex with her. He may love her body. He may love boasting to his buddies about his conquest. But he doesn't love her. True love will never ask the "beloved" to do what he or she thinks is wrong.

Love doesn't tear down the convictions of others. Quite the contrary.

"Love builds up" (1 Cor. 8:1).

"Whoever loves a brother or sister lives in the light and will not cause anyone to stumble" (1 John 2:10).

"You are sinning against Christ when you sin against other Christians by encouraging them to do something they believe is wrong" (1 Cor. 8:12 NLT).

Do you want to know if your love for someone is true? If your friendship is genuine? Check the room key. Ask yourself: Do I influence this person to do what is right?

If you answered yes, have some coffee. You're in the right hotel. If you want to be doubly sure, however, ask the next question.

Do I applaud what is right? For love "rejoices whenever the truth wins out" (1 Cor. 13:6 NLT).

The summer before my eighth-grade year I made friends with a guy named Larry. He was new to town, so I encouraged him to go out for our school football team. He could meet some guys, and being a stocky fellow, he might even make the squad. He agreed.

The result was a good news–bad news scenario. The good news? He made the cut. The bad news? He won my position. I was demoted to second string. I tried to be happy for him, but it was tough.

A few weeks into the season Larry fell off a motorcycle and broke a finger. I remember the day he stood at my front door holding up his bandaged hand. "Looks like you're going to have to play."

I tried to feel sorry for him, but it was hard. The passage was a lot easier for Paul to write than it was for me to practice. "Rejoice with those who rejoice, and weep with those who weep" (Rom. 12:15 NASB).

You want to plumb the depths of your love for someone? How do you feel when that person succeeds? Do you rejoice? Or are you jealous? And when he or she stumbles? Falls to misfortune? Are you really sorry? Or are you secretly pleased?

Love never celebrates misfortune. Never. I like the way Eugene Peterson translates the passage: "Love . . . doesn't revel when others grovel, [but] takes pleasure in the flowering of truth" (1 Cor. 13:6 MSG). J. B. Phillips is equally descriptive: "Love . . . does not . . . gloat over the wickedness of other people. On the contrary, it shares the joy of those who live by the truth."

You know your love is real when you weep with those who weep and rejoice with those who rejoice. You know your love is real when you feel for others what Catherine Lawes felt for the inmates of Sing Sing prison. When her husband, Lewis, became the warden in 1921, she was a young mother of three daughters. Everybody warned her never to step foot inside the walls. But she didn't listen to them. When the first prison basketball game was held, in she went, three girls in tow, and took a seat in the bleachers with the inmates.

She once said, "My husband and I are going to take care of these men, and I believe they will take care of me! I don't have to worry!"

When she heard that one convicted murderer was blind, she taught him Braille so he could read. Upon learning of inmates who were hearing impaired, she studied sign language so they could communicate. For sixteen years Catherine Lawes softened the hard hearts of the men of Sing Sing. In 1937 the world saw the difference real love makes.

The prisoners knew something was wrong when Lewis Lawes didn't report to work. Quickly the word spread that Catherine had been killed in a car accident. The following day her body was placed in her home, three-quarters of a mile from the prison. As the acting warden took his early morning walk, he noticed a large gathering at the main gate. Every prisoner pressed against the fence. Eyes awash with tears. Faces solemn. No one spoke or moved. They'd come to stand as close as they could to the woman who'd given them love.

The warden made a remarkable decision. "All right, men, you can go. Just be sure to check in tonight." These were America's hardest criminals. Murderers. Robbers. These were men the nation had locked away for life. But the warden unlocked the gate for them, and they walked without escort or guard to the home of Catherine Lawes to pay their last respects. And to a man, each one returned.[1]

Real love changes people.

Didn't God's love change you? Weren't you, like the prisoner, blind? You couldn't see beyond the grave. You couldn't see your purpose in life until he showed you. And you couldn't hear either. Oh, your ears functioned, but your heart didn't understand. You'd never heard of such love and kindness, and you never would have heard of it, but God spoke in your language. And, most of all, he set you free. You are free! Free to run away. Free to harden your heart. Free to duck down side streets and hide behind trash cans. But you don't. Or if you do, you come back. Why?

Because you've never been loved like this before.

God passes the test of 1 Corinthians 13:7. Does he want the best for you? "God himself does not tempt anyone" (James 1:13). Every action of heaven has one aim: that you know God. "He . . . made the earth hospitable, with plenty of time and space for living so we could seek after God, and not just grope around in the dark but actually find him" (Acts 17:26–27 MSG).

And does God rejoice when you do what is right? Certainly. "The LORD delights in those who fear him, who put their hope in his unfailing love" (Ps. 147:11 NIV). Does he weep when you do? Absolutely! He is the "God of all healing counsel! He comes alongside us when we go through hard times" (2 Cor. 1:3–4 MSG).

Do you want to know what love is? "This is what real love is: It is not our love for God; it is God's love for us in sending his Son to be the way to take away our sins" (1 John 4:10).

God passes the test. Well, he should; he drafted it.

So where does this leave us? Perhaps with a trio of reminders. When it comes to love:

Be careful. Make sure you're in the right hotel. Before you walk down the aisle, take a good long look around. Make sure this is God's intended place for you. And, if you suspect it isn't, get out. Don't force what is wrong to be right. Suppose I'd done that in the hotel. Suppose I'd demanded that the manager change the lock and the numbers on the door? I still would have been in the wrong place. Be careful.

And, until love is stirred, let God's love be enough for you. There are seasons when God allows us to feel the frailty of human love so we'll appreciate the strength of his love. Didn't he do this with David? Saul turned on him. Michal, his wife, betrayed him. Jonathan and Samuel were David's friends, but they couldn't follow him into the wilderness. Betrayal and circumstances left David alone. Alone with God. And, as David discovered, God was enough. David wrote these words in a desert: "Because your love is better than life, my lips will glorify you. . . . My soul will be satisfied as with the richest of foods" (Ps. 63:3, 5 NIV).

Be prayerful. What if it's too late? Specifically, what if you're married to someone you don't love—or who doesn't love you? Many choose to leave. That may be the step you take. But if it is, take at least a thousand others first. And bathe every one of those steps in prayer. Love is a fruit of the Spirit. Ask God to help you love as he loves. "God has given us the Holy Spirit, who fills our hearts with his love" (Rom. 5:5 CEV). Ask everyone you know to pray for you. Your friends. Your family. Your church leaders. Get your name on every prayer list available. And, most of all, pray for and, if possible, with your spouse. Ask the same God who raised the dead to resurrect the embers of your love.

Be grateful. Be grateful for those who love you. Be grateful for those who have encouraged you to do what is right and applauded when you did. Do you have people like that in your world? If so, you are doubly blessed. Be grateful for them. And be grateful for your Father in heaven. He passes the test with ease.

Isn't it good to know that even when we don't love with a perfect love, he does? God always nourishes what is right. He always applauds what is right. He has never done wrong, led one person to do wrong, or rejoiced when anyone did wrong. For he is love, and love "does not rejoice in unrighteousness, but rejoices with the truth" (1 Cor. 13:6 NASB).

LOVE IS A
PACKAGE DEAL

*Love . . . bears all things, believes all things,
hopes all things, endures all things.*

1 CORINTHIANS 13:4–7 NASB

How long must I put up with you?

Jesus' actions answered his own question. . . .

Until the rooster sings and the sweat stings and the

mallet rings

and a hillside of demons smirk at a dying God.

How long? Long enough for every sin to so soak my sinless soul

that heaven will turn in horror

until my swollen lips pronounce the final transaction: "It is

finished."

How long? Until it kills me.

My parents were not too big on restaurants. Partly because of the selection in our small town. Dairy Queen offered the gourmet selection, and everything went downhill from there. The main reason, though, was practicality. Why eat out when you can stay home? Restaurant trips were a Sunday-only, once-or-twice-a-month event. Funny, now that I am a parent, the philosophy is just the opposite. Why stay home when you can go out? (We tell our daughters it's time to eat, and they head for the garage.)

But when I was growing up, we typically ate at home. And every time we ate at home, my mom gave my brother and me the same instructions: "Put a little bit of everything on your plate."

We never had to be told to clean the plate. Eating volume was not a challenge. Variety was. Don't get me wrong, Mom was a good cook. But boiled okra? Asparagus? More like "croak-ra" and "gasp-aragus." Were they really intended for human consumption?

According to Mom, they were, and—according to Mom—they had to be eaten. "Eat some of everything." That was the rule in our house.

But that was not the rule at the cafeteria. On special occasions we made the forty-five-minute drive to the greatest culinary innovation since the gas stove: the cafeteria line. Ah, what a fine moment indeed to take a tray and gaze down the midway at the endless options. A veritable cornucopia of fine cuisine. Down the row you walk, intoxicated by the selection and liberated by the freedom. Yes to the fried fish; no to the fried tomatoes. Yes to the pecan pie; no, no, a thousand times no to the "croak-ra" and "gasp-ara-gus." Cafeteria lines are great.

Wouldn't it be nice if love were like a cafeteria line? What if you could look at the person with whom you live and select what you want and pass on what you don't? What if parents could do this with kids? "I'll take a plate of good grades and cute smiles, and I'm passing on the teenage identity crisis and tuition bills."

What if kids could do the same with parents? "Please give me a helping of allowances and free lodging but no rules or curfews, thank you."

And spouse with spouse? "H'm, how about a bowl of good health and good moods. But job transfers, in-laws, and laundry are not on my diet."

Wouldn't it be great if love were like a cafeteria line? It would be easier. It would be neater. It would be painless and peaceful. But you know what? It wouldn't be love. Love doesn't accept just a few things. Love is willing to accept all things.

"Love . . . bears all things, believes all things, hopes all things, endures all things" (1 Cor. 13:4–7 NKJV).

The apostle is looking for a ribbon to wrap around one of the sweetest paragraphs in Scripture. I envision the leathery-faced saint pausing in his dictation. "Let me think for a moment." Checking off his fingers, he reviews his list. "Let's see, patience, kindness, envy, arrogance. We've mentioned rudeness, selfishness, and anger, forgiveness, evil, and truth. Have I covered all things? Ah, that's it—all things. Here, write this down. Love bears all things, believes all things, hopes all things, endures all things."

Paul was never more the wordsmith than when he crafted this sentence. Listen to its rhythm as originally written: *panta stegei, panta pisteuei, panta elpigei, panta upomenei.* (Now when people ask you what you are doing, you can say, "I'm reading some Greek." Say it humbly, however, for love does not boast.) Did you notice the fourfold appearance of *panta*?

Expansions of *panta* appear in your English dictionary. *Pantheism* is the belief that God is in all things. A *pantry* is a cupboard where one can, hopefully, store all things. A *panacea* is a cure for all things. And a *panoply* is an array of all things. *Panta* means "all things."

God's view of love is like my mom's view of food. When we love someone, we take the entire package. No picking and choosing. No large helpings of the good and passing on the bad. Love is a package deal.

But how can we love those we find difficult to love?

The apostle Paul faced that same question. In fact, that's the reason we have this epistle. The church he began in southern Greece had gone wacko. When it came to unity, the members of the church in Corinth were out of step with each other. The apostle has barely placed pen on parchment before he writes:

> I appeal to you, brethren, by the name of our Lord Jesus Christ, that all of you agree and that there be no dissensions among you, but that you be united in the same mind and the same judgment. For it has been reported to me by Chloe's people that there is quarreling among you, my brethren. (1 Cor. 1:10–11 RSV)

The Greek word for *quarreling* also described battles in war. The Corinthian congregation was at war. Why? They couldn't agree on a leader. "One of you says, 'I follow Paul'; another says, 'I follow Apollos'; another says, 'I follow Peter'; and another says, 'I follow Christ'" (v. 12).

The church members had their favorite leaders. Some rallied around Paul, the church founder. Others liked Apollos, a dynamic speaker. Some preferred Peter, one of the original apostles. Some followed him, and others were happy just to follow Jesus. The congregation was divided into four groups, drawn and quartered into the Paulites, Apollosites, Peterites, and Jesusites. When it came to unity, the members were out of step.

When it came to morals, the church was out of control. Paul writes:

> I can hardly believe the report about the sexual immorality going on among you, something so evil that even the pagans don't do it. I am told that you have a man in your church who is living in sin with his father's wife. And you are so proud of yourselves! Why aren't you mourning in sorrow and shame? And why haven't you removed this man from your fellowship? (1 Cor. 5:1–2 NLT)

Paul wonders what is worse—the activity of the man or the apathy of the church?

One man was having an affair with his father's wife. Since Paul makes no mention of incest, the woman was likely his stepmother. Even the Corinthian society rebuffed such behavior. Roman law prohibited a son from marrying his father's wife, even if the father had died.[1] But smack-dab in the middle of the church, an interfamily affair was taking place, and no one was saying anything!

When it came to morals, the church was out of control. Their moral depravity likely resulted from their shallow theology, for when it came to biblical knowledge, the church was out of line.

The controversy was this: Can we eat meat that has been offered to idols? Pagan worship, like Jewish, involved the sacrifice of animals. Only a portion of the sacrifice was actually burned. The rest was divided between the priests and the public. Could Christians eat such meat?

The pro-meats said yes. After all, as Paul says, "We all know that an idol is not really a god and that there is only one God and no other" (1 Cor. 8:4 NLT). The pro-meats saw no problem with eating the meat.

The anti-meats, however, had a conscience problem. Paul uses verse 7 to put their dilemma in words: "Some are accustomed to thinking of idols as being real, so when they eat food that has been offered to idols, they think of it as the worship of real gods, and their weak consciences are violated" (NLT).

Some members felt that eating idol-offered meat endorsed idol worship. The anti-meats had a hard time making the break. And the pro-meats had a hard time being patient. They felt free in Christ and couldn't understand why others didn't feel the same.

Paul agrees with their conviction: "We don't miss out on anything if we don't eat it, and we don't gain anything if we do" (8:8 NLT). He had no trouble with the belief of the pro-meaters. But he had a lot of trouble with their arrogance. It's hard to miss the sarcasm of verse 2: "You think that everyone should agree with your perfect knowledge. While knowledge may make us feel important, it is love that really builds up the church. Anyone who claims to know all the answers doesn't really know very much" (8:1–2 NLT).

Ouch. The people had the right information but the wrong approach. They were too sophisticated for their own good.

Let's tally up the Corinthian confusion. Regarding unity, they were out of step. In terms of morality, they were out of control. Theologically, they were out of line.

But there's more! In the area of worship the church was way out of order. Just as their newfound freedom got them in trouble with morals and meat, it caused problems in the assembly.

Veils were a problem. Some of the women were coming to church without one. In Corinth, a veil was a sign of modesty and virtue. To appear unveiled in public was nothing short of immoral. The "enlightened" believers wanted to chuck the veils and "face" the future. Others, however, said, "Not so fast." Paul was one of them. The unveiled woman might as well shave her head, he argues (11:5). As long as she is going to attract attention to herself, why hold back?

And then there was the matter of the Lord's Supper. In Corinth the meal was more than crackers and juice; it was an extended time of food, fellowship, and worship. But some of the members were missing the point. They liked the food but disregarded the fellowship and worship. They arrived early and ate heartily, leaving nothing for the others but an empty table.

The women were missing the point with the veil. The others were missing the point with communion. And all of them were missing the point with the gifts of the Spirit. Some were proud of their gifts; others felt shortchanged. There was too much tongue speaking and preaching and not enough interpretation and listening, resulting in pandemonium (14:23).

Oh, Corinth. You have a problem on every pew! Territorially selfish. Morally shameless. Theologically reckless. And corporately thoughtless. How do you help a congregation like that?

You can correct them. Paul does. You can instruct them, which Paul does. You can reason with them; Paul does. But at some point, you stop talking to the head and start appealing to the heart.

And Paul does that: "Love . . . bears all things, believes all things, hopes all things, endures all things" (13:4–7 NKJV).

You parents can relate to Paul's problem. You've been there. From your daughter's bedroom comes a bloodcurdling cry. You rush to find your eight-year-old son yelling and his six-year-old sister tear streaked. You sigh, "What happened?" You never should have asked.

"He threw my Baby-Don't-Potty out the window."

"Well, she stepped on my WWF Nintendo game."

And off they go. He did. She did. She did. He did. You shake your head and wonder why your kids couldn't have been blessed with more traits from your side of the family.

Finally you make a "T" with your hands and shout, "Time out!" Forget the problems. You're going to the heart of the matter. You speak to your kids about something higher than toys, something grander than games. You speak to them about love. You speak to them about family. You dry her tears and stroke his head and wax eloquent on the topic of families' sticking together and looking out for each other. You tell them that life is too short for fights, and people are too precious for anger, and in the end the only thing that really solves it all is love.

They listen. They nod. And you are flooded with a fine feeling of satisfaction. You stand and then leave. The fighting could start again. But at least you planted the seed.

Paul could say the same. For twelve chapters, he's wrestled to untie the knots of disunity. For three more chapters, he'll try to make sense out of their conflicts. But chapter thirteen is his "Time out!" He sees only one solution. And that solution is a five-letter Greek word: A-G-A-P-E. *Agape.*

Paul could have used the Greek word *eros.* But he's not speaking of sexual love. He could have used the term *phileo,* but he presents far more than friendship. Or he could have used *storge,* a tender term for the love of family. But Paul has more in mind than domestic peace.

He envisions an *agape* love. *Agape* love cares for others because God has cared for us. *Agape* love goes beyond sentiment and good wishes. Because God loved first, *agape* love responds. Because God was gracious, *agape* love forgives the mistake when the offense is high. *Agape* offers patience when stress is abundant and extends kindness when kindness is rare. Why? Because God offered both to us.

Agape love "bears all things, believes all things, hopes all things, endures all things" (13:7 NKJV).

This is the type of love that Paul prescribes for the church in Corinth. Don't we need the same prescription today? Don't groups still fight with each other? Don't we flirt with those we shouldn't? Aren't we sometimes quiet when we should speak? And don't those who have found freedom still have the hardest time with those who haven't? Someday there will be a community where everyone behaves and no one complains. But it won't be this side of heaven.

So till then what do we do? We reason. We confront. We teach. But most of all we love.

Such love isn't easy. Not for you. Not for me. Not even for Jesus. Want proof? Listen to his frustration: "You people have no faith. How long must I stay with you? How long must I put up with you?" (Mark 9:19).

Even the Son of God was handed plates of "croak-ra" and "gasp-aragus." To know Jesus asked such a question reassures us. But to hear how he answered it will change us. *How long must I put up with you?*

"Long enough to be called crazy by my brothers and a liar by my neighbors. Long enough to be run out of my town and my Temple. Long enough to be laughed at, cursed, slapped, hit, blindfolded, and mocked. Long enough to feel warm spit and sharp whips and see my own blood puddle at my feet."

How long? "Until the rooster sings and the sweat stings and the mallet rings and a hillside of demons smirk at a dying God."

How long? "Long enough for every sin to so soak my sinless soul that heaven will turn in horror until my swollen lips pronounce the final transaction: 'It is finished.'"

How long? "Until it kills me."

Jesus bore all things, believed all things, hoped all things, and endured all things. Every single one.

A CLOAK OF LOVE

Love . . . always protects.

1 CORINTHIANS 13:6–7 NIV

W E HIDE. HE SEEKS.

WE BRING SIN. HE BRINGS A SACRIFICE.

WE TRY FIG LEAVES. HE BRINGS THE ROBE OF RIGHTEOUSNESS.

AND WE ARE LEFT TO SING THE SONG OF THE PROPHET:

"HE HAS COVERED ME WITH CLOTHES OF SALVATION

   AND WRAPPED ME WITH A COAT OF GOODNESS,

LIKE A BRIDEGROOM DRESSED FOR HIS WEDDING,

   LIKE A BRIDE DRESSED IN JEWELS" (ISA. 61:10).

In the 1930s, Joe Wise was a young, single resident at Cook Hospital in Fort Worth, Texas. Patients called him the "doctor with the rose." He made them smile by pinning a flower from bedside bouquets on his lab coat.

Madge, however, needed more than a smile. The automobile accident had left her leg nearly severed at the knee. She was young, beautiful, and very much afraid. When Joe spotted her in the ER, he did something he'd never done before.

Joe took his lab coat, bejeweled with the rose, and placed it gently over the young woman. As she was wheeled into the operating room, the coat was removed, but she asked to keep the flower. When she awoke from surgery, it was still in her hand.

When I tell you that Madge never forgot Joe, you won't be surprised. When I tell you how she thanked him, you very well may be.

But before we finish the story of Joe's cloak, could I ask you to think about your own? Do you own a cloak of love? Do you know anyone who needs one? When you cover someone with concern, you are fulfilling what

Paul had in mind when he wrote the phrase "love . . . always protects" (1 Cor. 13:4–7 NIV).

Paul employed a rich word here. Its root meaning is "to cover or conceal." Its cousins on the noun side of the family are *roof* and *shelter*. When Paul said, "Love always protects," he might have been thinking of the shade of a tree or the refuge of a house. He might even have been thinking of a coat. One scholar thinks he was. The *Theological Dictionary of the New Testament* is known for its word study, not its poetry. But the scholar sounds poetic as he explains the meaning of *protect* as used in 1 Corinthians 13:7. The word conveys, he says, "the idea of covering with a cloak of love."[1]

Remember receiving one? You were nervous about the test, but the teacher stayed late to help you. You were far from home and afraid, but your mother phoned to comfort you. You were innocent and accused, so your friend stood to defend you. Covered with encouragement. Covered with tender-hearted care. Covered with protection. *Covered with a cloak of love.*

Your finest cloak of love, however, came from God. Never thought of your Creator as a clothier? Adam and Eve did.

Every clothing store in the world owes its existence to Adam and Eve. Ironing boards, closets, hangers—all trace their ancestry back to the Garden of Eden. Before Adam and Eve sinned, they needed no clothing; after they sinned, they couldn't get dressed fast enough. They hid in the bushes and set about the task of making a wardrobe out of fig leaves.

They craved protection. Well they should have. They knew the consequences of their mistake. God had warned them, "You must not eat fruit from the tree that is in the middle of the garden. You must not even touch it, or you will die" (Gen. 3:3).

Of course the one tree they were told not to touch was the one they couldn't resist, and the fruit of the tree became a doorknob that, once pulled, permitted a slew of unwanted consequences to enter.

One of which was shame. Adam and Eve had felt no shame. Then they felt nothing but. Hence they hid, and hence they sewed, but the covering was insufficient. What is a grove of trees to the eyes of God? What protection is found in a fig leaf?

Adam and Eve found themselves, like Madge, vulnerable on a gurney— wounded, not by a car, but by their own sin.

But what would God do? Had he not announced his judgment? Hadn't his law been broken? Didn't justice demand their death? Is he not righteous?

But, we are quick to counter, is God not love? And weren't Adam and Eve his children? Could his mercy override his justice? Is there some way that righteousness can coexist with kindness?

According to Genesis 3:21 it can. The verse has been called the first gospel sermon. Preached not by preachers, but by God himself. Not with words, but with symbol and action. You want to see how God responds to our sin?

"The LORD God made clothes from animal skins for the man and his wife and dressed them" (Gen. 3:21).

The mystery behind those words! Read them again, and try to envision the moment.

"The LORD God made clothes from animal skins for the man and his wife and dressed them."

That simple sentence suggests three powerful scenes.

Scene 1: God slays an animal. For the first time in the history of the earth, dirt is stained with blood. Innocent blood. The beast committed no sin. The creature did not deserve to die.

Adam and Eve did. The couple deserve to die, but they live. The animal deserves to live, but it dies. In scene 1, innocent blood is shed.

Scene 2: Clothing is made. The shaper of the stars now becomes a tailor. And in Scene 3: God dresses them. "The LORD . . . dressed them."

Oh, for a glimpse of that moment. Adam and Eve are on their way out of the garden. They've been told to leave, but now God tells them to stop. "Those fig leaves," he says, shaking his head, "will never do." And he produces some clothing. But he doesn't throw the garments at their feet and tell them to get dressed. He dresses them himself. "Hold still, Adam. Let's see how this fits." As a mother would dress a toddler. As a father would zip up the jacket of a preschooler. As a physician would place a lab coat over a frightened girl. God covers them. He protects them.

Love always protects.

Hasn't he done the same for us? We eat our share of forbidden fruit. We say what we shouldn't say. Go where we shouldn't go. Pluck fruit from trees we shouldn't touch.

And when we do, the door opens, and the shame tumbles in. And we hide. We sew fig leaves. Flimsy excuses. See-through justifications. We cover ourselves in good works and good deeds, but one gust of the wind of truth, and we are naked again—stark naked in our own failure.

So what does God do? Exactly what he did for our parents in the garden. He sheds innocent blood. He offers the life of his Son. And from the scene of the sacrifice the Father takes a robe—not the skin of an animal—but the robe of righteousness. And does he throw it in our direction and tell us to shape up? No, he dresses us himself. He dresses us *with* himself. "You were all baptized into Christ, and so you were all clothed with Christ" (Gal. 3:26–27).

The robing is his work, not ours. Did you note the inactivity of Adam and Eve? They did nothing. Absolutely nothing. They didn't request the sacrifice; they didn't think of the sacrifice; they didn't even dress themselves. They were passive in the process. So are we. "You have been saved by grace through believing. You did not save yourselves; it was a gift from God. It was not the result of your own efforts, so you cannot brag about it. God has made us what we are" (Eph. 2:8–10).

We hide. He seeks. We bring sin. He brings a sacrifice. We try fig leaves. He brings the robe of righteousness. And we are left to sing the song of the prophet: "He has covered me with clothes of salvation and wrapped me with a coat of goodness, like a bridegroom dressed for his wedding, like a bride dressed in jewels" (Isa. 61:10).

God has clothed us. He protects us with a cloak of love. Can you look back over your life and see instances of God's protection? I can too. My junior year in college I was fascinated by a movement of Christians several thousand miles from my campus. Some of my friends decided to spend the summer at the movement's largest church and be discipled. When I tried to do the same, every door closed. Problem after problem with finances, logistics, and travel.

A second opportunity surfaced: spending a summer in Brazil. In this case, every door I knocked on swung open. Two and one half decades later I see how God protected me. The movement has become a cult—dangerous and oppressive. Time in Brazil introduced me to grace—freeing and joyful. Did God protect me? Does God protect us?

Does he do for us what he did for the woman caught in adultery? He protected her from the stones. And his disciples? He protected them from the storm. And the demoniac? He protected him from hell itself. Why, Jesus even protected Peter from the tax collectors by providing a tax payment.[2]

And you? Did he keep you from a bad relationship? Protect you from the wrong job? Insulate you from _____ (you fill in the blank)? "Like hovering birds, so will [the LORD Almighty] protect Jerusalem" (Isa. 31:5 JB). "He will strengthen and protect you" (2 Thess. 3:3 NIV). "He will command his angels . . . to guard you" (Ps. 91:11 NIV). God protects you with a cloak of love.

Wouldn't you love to do the same for him? What if you were given the privilege of Mary? What if God himself were placed in your arms as a naked baby? Would you not do what she did? "She wrapped the baby with pieces of cloth" (Luke 2:7).

The baby Jesus, still wet from the womb, was cold and chilled. So this mother did what any mother would do; she did what love does: She covered him.

Three decades later another lover of Christ did the same. This time the body of Jesus wasn't cold from the chill; it was cold from death. Joseph of Arimathea had it lowered from the cross. Just as Mary cleansed the child from the womb, Joseph prepared the Savior for the tomb. He washed the spit from the face and sponged the blood from the beard. "Then Joseph took the body and wrapped it in a clean linen cloth" (Matt. 27:59).

Mary dressed the baby. Joseph cleansed the body.

Wouldn't you cherish an opportunity to do the same? You have one. Such opportunities come your way every day. Jesus said,

> "I was without clothes, and you gave me something to wear." . . .
>
> "When," [the people asked,] "did we see you without clothes and give you something to wear?" . . .
>
> "I tell you the truth, anything you did for even the least of my people here, you also did for me." (Matt. 25:36, 38, 40)

Do you know anyone, like Madge, who is wounded and afraid? Do you know anyone, like Adam and Eve, who is guilty and embarrassed? Do you know anyone who needs a cloak of love?

Have you ever had a teenager in trouble? You hear the garage door open after the curfew hour. You climb out of bed and march to the kitchen, and there you find him at the counter. The smell of beer is on his breath. The flush of alcohol is on his cheeks. This is serious. He has been drinking. He has been driving. You have a problem, and I have a question. What are you going to give your son?

Are you going to give him a lecture? He deserves one. Are you going to give him three months with no keys? That may be wise. Are you going to give him a life sentence with no parole? That may be understandable, considering your worry—but don't forget to give your child a cloak of love. At some point over the next few hours he desperately needs to feel your arm around his shoulders. He needs to be cloaked, covered, blanketed in your love. Love always protects.

Know anyone who needs a cloak of love?

Have you ever heard anyone gossip about someone you know? Ever seen human jackals make a meal out of a fallen friend? "Well, I heard that she . . ." "Oh, but didn't you know that she . . ." "Let me tell you what a friend told me about him . . ." Then all of a sudden it's your turn. Everybody is picking your friend apart. What do you have to say?

Here is what love says: Love says nothing. Love stays silent. "Love covers a multitude of sins" (1 Pet. 4:8 NASB). Love doesn't expose. It doesn't gossip. If love says anything, love speaks words of defense. Words of kindness. Words of protection.

Know anyone in need of a cloak of love?

A few years back I offered one to my daughters. The whirlwind of adolescence was making regular runs through our house, bringing with it more than our share of doubts, pimples, and peer pressure. I couldn't protect the girls from the winds, but I could give them an anchor to hold in the midst. On Valentine's Day, 1997, I wrote the following and had it framed for each daughter:

I have a special gift for you. My gift is warmth at night and sunlit afternoons, chuckles and giggles and happy Saturdays.

But how do I give this gift? Is there a store which sells laughter? A catalog that offers kisses? No. Such a treasure can't be bought. But it can be given. And here is how I give it to you.

Your Valentine's Day gift is a promise, a promise that I will always love your mother. With God as my helper, I will never leave her. You'll never come home to find me gone. You'll never wake up and find that I have run away. You'll always have two parents. I will love your mother. I will honor your mother. I will cherish your mother. That is my promise. That is my gift.

Love, Dad

Know anyone who could use some protection? Of course you do. Then give some.

Pay a gas bill for a struggling elderly couple.

Promise your kids that, God being your helper, they'll never know a hungry day or a homeless night.

Tell your husband that you'd do it all over again and invite him on a honeymoon.

Make sure your divorced friends are invited to your parties.

And when you see a wounded soul, shivering and shaken on a gurney of life, offer a lab coat and leave the rose.

That's what Dr. Wise did. And he didn't stop there. As Madge recovered, he paid visits to her room. Many visits. When he learned that she was engaged, he hung a "No Visitors" sign on her door so her fiancé couldn't enter. Madge didn't object. Her diary reads, "I hope that handsome young doctor comes by to visit today." He did, that day and many others, always with a rose. One a day until she was dismissed from the hospital.

And Madge never forgot. Her response? She gave him a rose in return. The next day she gave another. Then the next, another. As they started dating, the daily roses still came. When they married, she didn't stop giving them. Madge convinced the Colonial Golf Course across the street from her house to plant roses so she could give the doctor his daily gift. For nearly forty years, every day—a rose. Their younger son, Harold, says he can't remember a time when there wasn't a glass in the refrigerator containing roses for his dad.[3]

A cloak of love. A rose of gratitude.

Have you been given the first? Then take time to give the second.

CHAPTER
THIRTEEN

THE RING
OF BELIEF

Love . . . believes all things.

1 CORINTHIANS 13:4–7 NASB

WHEN YOU SPEAK TRUTH, YOU ARE GOD'S AMBASSADOR.

AS YOU STEWARD THE MONEY HE GIVES, YOU ARE HIS BUSINESS MANAGER.

WHEN YOU DECLARE FORGIVENESS, YOU ARE HIS PRIEST.

AS YOU STIR THE HEALING OF THE BODY OR THE SOUL, YOU ARE
HIS PHYSICIAN.

AND WHEN YOU PRAY, HE LISTENS TO YOU AS A FATHER LISTENS TO A SON.

YOU HAVE A VOICE IN THE HOUSEHOLD OF GOD. HE HAS GIVEN YOU
HIS RING.

By all rules, Skinner was a dead man." With these words Arthur Bressi begins his retelling of the day he found his best friend in a World War II Japanese concentration camp. The two were high-school buddies. They grew up together in Mount Carmel, Pennsylvania—playing ball, skipping school, double-dating. Arthur and Skinner were inseparable. It made sense, then, that when one joined the army, the other would as well. They rode the same troopship to the Philippines. That's where they were separated. Skinner was on Bataan when it fell to the Japanese in 1942. Arthur Bressi was captured a month later.

Through the prison grapevine, Arthur learned the whereabouts of his friend. Skinner was near death in a nearby camp. Arthur volunteered for work detail in the hope that his company might pass through the other camp. One day they did.

Arthur requested and was given five minutes to find and speak to his friend. He knew to go to the sick side of the camp. It was divided into two sections—one for those expected to recover, the other for those given no hope. Those expected to die lived in a barracks called "zero ward." That's where Arthur found Skinner. He called his name, and out of the barracks walked the seventy-nine-pound shadow of the friend he had once known.

As he writes:

> I stood at the wire fence of the Japanese prisoner-of-war camp on Luzon and watched my childhood buddy, caked in filth and racked with the pain of multiple diseases, totter toward me. He was dead; only his boisterous spirit hadn't left his body. I wanted to look away, but couldn't. His blue eyes, watery and dulled, locked on me and wouldn't let go.[1]

Malaria. Amebic dysentery. Pellagra. Scurvy. Beriberi. Skinner's body was a dormitory for tropical diseases. He couldn't eat. He couldn't drink. He was nearly gone.

Arthur didn't know what to do or say. His five minutes were nearly up. He began to finger the heavy knot of the handkerchief tied around his neck. In it was his high-school class ring. At the risk of punishment, he'd smuggled the ring into camp. Knowing the imminence of disease and the scarcity of treatment, he had been saving it to barter for medicine or food for himself. But one look at Skinner, and he knew he couldn't save it any longer.

As he told his friend good-bye, he slipped the ring through the fence into Skinner's frail hand and told him to "wheel and deal" with it. Skinner objected, but Arthur insisted. He turned and left, not knowing if he would ever see his friend alive again.

What kind of love would do something like that? It's one thing to give a gift to the healthy. It's one thing to share a treasure with the strong. But to give your best to the weak, to entrust your treasure to the dying—that's saying something. Indeed, that's saying something to them. "I believe in you," the gesture declares. "Don't despair. Don't give up. I believe in you." It's no wonder Paul included this phrase in his definition of love. "[Love] believes all things" (1 Cor. 13:7 NASB).

Do you know anyone who is standing on Skinner's side of the fence? If your child is having trouble in school, you do. If your husband struggles with depression or your wife has been laid off, you do. If you have a friend with cancer, if the class mocks your classmate, if your son doesn't make the squad, if you know anyone who is afraid or has failed or is frail, then you know someone who needs a ring of belief.

And, what's more, you can give them one. You may, by virtue of your words or ways, change that person's life forever.

Arthur did. Want to know what happened to Skinner? He took the ring and buried it in the barracks floor. The next day he took the biggest risk of his life. He approached the "kindest" of the guards and passed him the ring through the fence. *"Takai?"* the guard asked. "Is it valuable?" Skinner assured him that it was. The soldier smiled and slipped the ring into a pocket and left. A couple of days later he walked past Skinner and let a packet drop at his feet. Sulfanilamide tablets. A day later he returned with limes to combat the scurvy. Then came a new pair of pants and some canned beef. Within three weeks Skinner was on his feet. Within three months he was taken to the healthy side of the sick camp. In time he was able to work. As far as Skinner knew, he was the only American ever to leave the zero ward alive.

All because of a ring. All because someone believed in him.

I know what some of you are thinking. You're looking at Arthur and Skinner and wishing your situation were so easy. Skinner was a dying man but a good man, a good friend. How do you believe in someone who isn't? How do you believe in a man who cheats on you or an employee who swindles you? Does love ignore all things? I don't think so. This passage is not a call to naiveté or blindness. It is, however, a call for us to give to others what God has given us.

Skinner is not the only person to be given a ring, you know. You have one on your finger as well. Your heavenly Father placed it there. Jesus described the moment when he told the story of the prodigal son.

The tale involves a wealthy father and a willful son. The boy prematurely takes his inheritance and moves to Las Vegas and there wastes the money on slot machines and call girls. As fast as you can say "blackjack," he is broke. Too proud to go home, he gets a job sweeping horse stables at the racetrack. When he finds himself tasting some of their oats and thinking, *H'm, a dash of salt and this wouldn't be too bad,* he realizes enough is enough. It's time to go home. The gardener at his father's house does better than this. So off he goes, rehearsing his repentance speech every step of the way.

But the father has other ideas. "When he was still a great way off, his father saw him." The dad was looking for the boy, always craning his neck, ever hoping the boy would show, and when he did, when the father saw the familiar figure on the trail, he "had compassion, and ran and fell on his neck and kissed him."

We don't expect such a response. We expect crossed arms and a furrowed brow. At best a guarded handshake. At least a stern lecture. But the father gives none of these. Instead he gives gifts. "Bring out the best robe . . . a ring . . . sandals. . . . And bring the fatted calf . . . and let us eat and be merry" (Luke 15:11–23 NKJV). Robe, sandals, calf, and . . . Did you see it? A ring.

Before the boy has a chance to wash his hands, he has a ring to put on his finger. In Christ's day rings were more than gifts; they were symbols of delegated sovereignty. The bearer of the ring could speak on behalf of the giver. It was used to press a seal into soft wax to validate a transaction. The one who wore the ring conducted business in the name of the one who gave it.

Would you have done this? Would you have given this prodigal son power-of-attorney privileges over your affairs? Would you have entrusted him with a credit card? Would you have given him this ring?

Before you start questioning the wisdom of the father, remember, in this story you are the boy. When you came home to God, you were given authority to conduct business in your heavenly Father's name.

When you speak truth, you are God's ambassador.

As you steward the money he gives, you are his business manager.

When you declare forgiveness, you are his priest.

As you stir the healing of the body or the soul, you are his physician.

And when you pray, he listens to you as a father listens to a son. You have a voice in the household of God. He has given you his ring.

The only thing more remarkable than the giving of the ring is the fact that he hasn't taken it back! Weren't there times when he could have?

When you promoted your cause and forgot his. When you spoke lies and not truth. When you took his gifts and used them for personal gain. When you took the bus back to Las Vegas and found yourself seduced into the world of lights, luck, and long nights. Couldn't he have taken the ring? Absolutely. But did he? Do you still have a Bible? Are you still allowed to pray? Do you still have a dollar to manage or a skill to use? Then it appears that he still wants you to have the ring. It appears that he still believes in you!

He hasn't given up on you. He hasn't turned away. He hasn't walked out. He could have. Others would have. But he hasn't. God believes in you. And, I wonder, could you take some of the belief that he has in you and share it with someone else? Could you believe in someone?

There is such power in belief. Robert Schuller said, "I am not who I think I am. I am not who you think I am. I am who I think you think I am."[2] (You might want to read that twice.) Right or wrong, we define ourselves through other people's eyes. Tell me enough times that I'm stupid, and I'll believe you. Tell me enough times that I'm bright, and I might agree. Or as the German poet Goethe stated, "Treat a man as he appears to be, and you make him worse. But treat a man as if he were what he potentially could be, and you make him what he should be."

Robert Rosenthal demonstrated this in a famous classroom study. He and an elementary-school principal tested a group of students. They then mentioned to the students' teachers that some of the kids had done extremely well on the tests. The teachers were led to believe that five or six of the students had exceptional learning ability.

What the teachers did not know was that the names of the "exceptional" students had been chosen entirely at random. They were no different from the others, but since the teachers thought they were, the teachers treated them differently. By the end of the year the ones the teachers thought were brighter actually were! They scored ahead of their peers and gained as much as fifteen to twenty-seven IQ points. The teachers described the students as happier, more curious, more affectionate than the average, and having a better chance of success later in life. This was all due to the attitude of the teachers! The teachers thought the students were special, and the students lived up to their treatment. Rosenthal wrote:

> The explanation probably lies in the subtle interaction between teachers and pupils; tone of voice, facial expressions, touch and posture may be the means by which—often unwittingly—teachers communicate their expectations to their pupils. Such communication may help a child by changing his perception of himself.[3]

Arthur gave Skinner much more than a ring; he gave him a proclamation, a judgment that said, "You are worth this much to me! Your life is worth saving. Your life is worth living." He believed in him and, as a result, gave Skinner the means and the courage to save himself.

You and I have the privilege to do for others what Arthur did for Skinner and what God does for us. How do we show people that we believe in them?

Show up. Nothing takes the place of your presence. Letters are nice. Phone calls are special, but being there in the flesh sends a message.

After Albert Einstein's wife died, his sister, Maja, moved in to assist with the household affairs. For fourteen years she cared for him, allowing his valuable research to continue. In 1950 she suffered a stroke and lapsed into a coma. Thereafter, Einstein spent two hours every afternoon reading aloud to her from Plato.[4] She gave no sign of understanding his words, but he read anyway. If she understood anything by his gesture, she understood this—he believed that she was worth his time.

Do you believe in your kids? Then show up. Show up at their games. Show up at their plays. Show up at their recitals. It may not be possible to make each one, but it's sure worth the effort. An elder in our church supports me with his presence. Whenever I speak at an area congregation, he'll show up. Does nothing. Says little. Just takes a seat in a pew and smiles when we make eye contact. It means a lot to me. In fact, as I write the final draft of this book, he is one room away. Made the ninety-minute drive from his house to my hideout just to pray for me. Do you believe in your friends? Then show up. Show up at their graduations and weddings. Spend time with them. You want to bring out the best in someone? Then show up.

Listen up. You don't have to speak to encourage. The Bible says, "It is best to listen much, speak little" (James 1:19 TLB). We tend to speak much and listen little. There is a time to speak. But there is also a time to be quiet. That's what my father did. Dropping a fly ball may not be a big deal to most people, but if you are thirteen years old and have aspirations of the big leagues, it is a big deal. Not only was it my second error of the game, it allowed the winning run to score.

I didn't even go back to the dugout. I turned around in the middle of left field and climbed over the fence. I was halfway home when my dad found me. He didn't say a word. Just pulled over to the side of the road, leaned across the seat, and opened the passenger door. We didn't speak. We didn't need to. We both knew the world had come to an end. When we got home, I went straight to my room, and he went straight to the kitchen. Presently he appeared in front of me with cookies and milk. He took a seat on the bed, and we broke bread together. Somewhere in the dunking of the cookies I began to realize that life and my father's love would go on. In the economy of male adolescence, if you love the guy who drops the ball, then you really love him. My skill as a baseball player didn't improve, but my confidence in Dad's love did. Dad never said a word. But he did show up. He did listen up. To bring out the best in others, do the same, and then, when appropriate:

Speak up. Nathaniel Hawthorne came home heartbroken. He'd just been fired from his job in the custom house. His wife, rather than responding with anxiety, surprised him with joy. "Now you can write your book!"

He wasn't so positive. "And what shall we live on while I'm writing it?"

To his amazement she opened a drawer and revealed a wad of money she'd saved out of her housekeeping budget. "I always knew you were a man of genius," she told him. "I always knew you'd write a masterpiece."

She believed in her husband. And because she did, he wrote. And because he wrote, every library in America has a copy of *The Scarlet Letter* by Nathaniel Hawthorne.[5]

You have the power to change someone's life simply by the words that you speak. "Death and life are in the power of the tongue" (Prov. 18:21 NKJV). That's why Paul urges you and me to be careful. "When you talk, do not say harmful things, but say what people need—words that will help others become stronger" (Eph. 4:29).

Earlier I gave you a test for love. There's also a test for the tongue. Before you speak, ask: Will what I'm about to say help others become stronger? You have the ability, with your words, to make a person stronger. Your words are to their soul what a vitamin is to their body. If you had food and saw someone starving, would you not share it? If you had water and saw someone dying of thirst, would you not give it? Of course you would. Then won't you do the same for their hearts? Your words are food and water! Do not withhold encouragement from the discouraged. Do not keep affirmation from the beaten down! Speak words that make people stronger. Believe in them as God has believed in you.

You may save someone's life.

Arthur did. His friend Skinner survived. Both men returned home to Mount Carmel. One day, soon after their arrival, Skinner came over for a visit. He had a gift with him. A small box. Arthur knew immediately what it was. It was an exact copy of the high-school ring. After a lame attempt at humor—"Don't lose that; it cost me eighteen dollars"—he gave his friend a warm smile and said, "That ring, Artie . . . it saved my life."[6]

May someone say the same to you.

May you say the same to God.

FOURTEEN

WHEN YOU'RE
LOW ON HOPE

Love . . . always hopes.

1 CORINTHIANS 13:7 NIV

Hope is an olive leaf—evidence of dry land after a flood.

Proof to the dreamer that dreaming is worth the risk.

W ater. All Noah can see is water. The evening sun sinks into it. The clouds are reflected in it. His boat is surrounded by it. Water. Water to the north. Water to the south. Water to the east. Water to the west. Water.

All Noah can see is water.

He can't remember when he's seen anything but. He and the boys had barely pushed the last hippo up the ramp when heaven opened a thousand fire hydrants. Within moments the boat was rocking, and for days the rain was pouring, and for weeks Noah has been wondering, *How long is this going to last?* For forty days it rained. For months they have floated. For months they have eaten the same food, smelled the same smell, and looked at the same faces. After a certain point you run out of things to say to each other.

Finally the boat bumped, and the rocking stopped. Mrs. Noah gave Mr. Noah a look, and Noah gave the hatch a shove and poked his head through. The hull of the ark was resting on ground, but the ground was still surrounded by water. "Noah," she yelled up at him, "what do you see?"

"Water."

He sent a raven on a scouting mission; it never returned. He sent a dove. It came back shivering and spent, having found no place to roost. Then, just this morning, he tried again. He pulled a dove out of the bowels of the ark and ascended the ladder. The morning sun caused them both to squint. As he kissed the breast of the bird, he felt a pounding heart. Had he put a hand on his chest, he would have felt another. With a prayer he let it go and watched until the bird was no bigger than a speck on a window.

All day he looked for the dove's return. In between chores he opened the hatch and searched. The boys wanted him to play a little pin the tail on the donkey, but he passed. He chose instead to climb into the crow's-nest and look. The wind lifted his gray hair. The sun warmed his weather-beaten face. But nothing lifted his heavy heart. He had seen nothing. Not in the morning. Not after lunch. Not later.

Now the sun is setting, and the sky is darkening, and he has come to look one final time, but all he sees is water. Water to the north. Water to the south. Water to the east. Water to the . . .

You know the feeling. You have stood where Noah stood. You've known your share of floods. Flooded by sorrow at the cemetery, stress at the office, anger at the disability in your body or the inability of your spouse. You've seen the floodwater rise, and you've likely seen the sun set on your hopes as well. You've been on Noah's boat.

And you've needed what Noah needed; you've needed some hope. You're not asking for a helicopter rescue, but the sound of one would be nice. Hope doesn't promise an instant solution but rather the possibility of an eventual one. Sometimes all we need is a little hope.

That's all Noah needed. And that's all Noah received.

The old sailor stares at the sun bisected by the horizon. Could hardly imagine a more beautiful sight. But he'd give this one and a hundred more for an acre of dry ground and a grove of grapes. Mrs. Noah's voice reminds him that dinner is on the table and he should lock the hatch, and he's just about to call it a day when he hears the cooing of the dove. Here is how the Bible describes the moment: "When the dove returned to him in the evening, there in its beak was a freshly plucked olive leaf!" (Gen. 8:11 NIV).

An olive leaf. Noah would have been happy to have the bird but to have the leaf! This leaf was more than foliage; this was promise. The bird brought more than a piece of a tree; it brought hope. For isn't that what hope is? Hope is an olive leaf—evidence of dry land after a flood. Proof to the dreamer that dreaming is worth the risk.

Don't we love the olive leaves of life?

"It appears the cancer may be in remission."

"I can help you with those finances."

"We'll get through this together."

What's more, don't we love the doves that bring them? When the father walks his son through his first broken heart, he gives him an olive leaf. When the wife of many years consoles the wife of a few months, when she tells her that conflicts come and all husbands are moody and these storms pass, you know what she is doing? She is giving an olive leaf.

We love olive leaves. And we love those who give them.

Perhaps that's the reason so many loved Jesus.

He stands near a woman who was yanked from a bed of promiscuity. She's still dizzy from the raid. A door slammed open, covers were pulled back, and the fraternity of moral police barged in. And now here she stands. Noah could see nothing but water. She can see nothing but anger. She has no hope.

But then Jesus speaks, "If any one of you is without sin, let him be the first to throw a stone at her" (John 8:7 NIV). Silence. Both the eyes and the rocks of the accusers hit the ground. Within moments they have left, and Jesus is alone with the woman. The dove of heaven offers her a leaf.

"Woman, where are they? Has no one condemned you?"

"No one, sir," she said.

"Then neither do I condemn you," Jesus declared. "Go now and leave your life of sin." (vv. 10–11 NIV)

Into her shame-flooded world he brings a leaf of hope.

He does something similar for Martha. She is bobbing in a sea of sorrow. Her brother is dead. His body has been buried. And Jesus, well, Jesus is late. "If you had been here, my brother would not have died." Then I think she might have paused. "But I know that even now God will give you whatever you ask" (John 11:21–22 NIV). As Noah opened his hatch, so Martha opens her heart. As the dove brought a leaf, so Christ brings the same.

"I am the resurrection and the life. He who believes in me will live, even though he dies; and whoever lives and believes in me will never die. Do you believe this?"

"Yes, Lord," she told him, "I believe that you are the Christ, the Son of God, who was to come into the world." (John 11:25–27 NIV)

How could he get by with such words? Who was he to make such a claim? What qualified him to offer grace to one woman and a promise of resurrection to another? Simple. He had done what the dove did. He'd crossed the shoreline of the future land and journeyed among the trees. And from the grove of grace he plucked a leaf for the woman. And from the tree of life he pulled a sprig for Martha.

And from both he brings leaves to you. Grace and life. Forgiveness of sin. The defeat of death. This is the hope he gives. This is the hope we need.

In his book *The Grand Essentials,* Ben Patterson tells of an S-4 submarine that sank off the coast of Massachusetts. The entire crew was trapped.

Every effort was made to rescue the sailors, but every effort failed. Near the end of the ordeal, a deep-sea diver heard tapping on the steel wall of the sunken sub. As he placed his helmet against the vessel, he realized he was hearing a sailor tap out this question in Morse code: "Is there any hope?"[1]

To the guilty that ask that question, Jesus says, "Yes!"

To the death-struck that ask that question, Jesus answers, "Yes!"

To all the Noahs of the world, to all who search the horizon for a fleck of hope, he proclaims, "Yes!" And he comes. He comes as a dove. He comes bearing fruit from a distant land, from our future home. He comes with a leaf of hope.

Have you received yours? Don't think your ark is too isolated. Don't think your flood is too wide. Your toughest challenge is nothing more than bobby pins and rubber bands to God. *Bobby pins and rubber bands?*

My older sister used to give them to me when I was a child. I would ride my tricycle up and down the sidewalk, pretending that the bobby pins were keys and my trike was a truck. But one day I lost the "keys." Crisis! What was I going to do? My search yielded nothing but tears and fear. But when I confessed my mistake to my sister, she just smiled. Being a decade older, she had a better perspective.

God has a better perspective as well. With all due respect, our severest struggles are, in his view, nothing worse than lost bobby pins and rubber bands. He is not confounded, confused, or discouraged.

Receive his hope, won't you? Receive it because you need it. Receive it so you can share it.

What do you suppose Noah did with his? What do you think he did with the leaf? Did he throw it overboard and forget about it? Do you suppose he stuck it in his pocket and saved it for a scrapbook? Or do you think he let out a whoop and assembled the troops and passed it around like the Hope Diamond it was?

Certainly he whooped. That's what you do with hope. What do you do with olive leaves? You pass them around. You don't stick them in your pocket. You give them to the ones you love. Love always hopes. "Love . . . bears all things, believes all things, *hopes* all things, endures all things" (1 Cor. 13:4–7 NKJV, emphasis mine).

Love has hope in you.

The aspiring young author was in need of hope. More than one person had told him to give up. "Getting published is impossible," one mentor said. "Unless you are a national celebrity, publishers won't talk to you." Another warned, "Writing takes too much time. Besides, you don't want all your thoughts on paper."

Initially he listened. He agreed that writing was a waste of effort and turned his attention to other projects. But somehow the pen and pad were bourbon and Coke to the wordaholic. He'd rather write than read. So he wrote. How many nights did he pass on that couch in the corner of the apartment reshuffling his deck of verbs and nouns? And how many hours did his wife sit with him? He wordsmithing. She cross-stitching. Finally a manuscript was finished. Crude and laden with mistakes but finished.

She gave him the shove. "Send it out. What's the harm?"

So out it went. Mailed to fifteen different publishers. While the couple waited, he wrote. While he wrote, she stitched. Neither expecting much, both hoping everything. Responses began to fill the mailbox. "I'm sorry, but we don't accept unsolicited manuscripts." "We must return your work. Best of luck." "Our catalog doesn't have room for unpublished authors."

I still have those letters. Somewhere in a file. Finding them would take some time. Finding Denalyn's cross-stitch, however, would take none. To see it, all I do is lift my eyes from this monitor and look on the wall. "Of all those arts in which the wise excel, nature's chief masterpiece is writing well."

She gave it to me about the time the fifteenth letter arrived. A publisher had said yes. That letter is also framed. Which of the two is more meaningful? The gift from my wife or the letter from the publisher? The gift, hands down. For in giving the gift, Denalyn gave hope.

Love does that. Love extends an olive leaf to the loved one and says, "I have hope in you."

Love is just as quick to say, "I have hope *for* you."

You can say those words. You are a flood survivor. By God's grace you have found your way to dry land. You know what it's like to see the waters subside. And since you do, since you passed through a flood and lived to tell about it, you are qualified to give hope to someone else.

What? Can't think of any floods in your past? Let me jog your memory. How about adolescence? Remember the torrent of the teenage years? Remember the hormones and hemlines? The puberty and pimples? Those were tough times. *Yeah,* you're thinking, *but you get through them.* That's exactly what teenagers need to hear you say. They need an olive leaf from a survivor.

So do young couples. It happens in every marriage. The honeymoon ends, and the river of romance becomes the river of reality, and they wonder if they will survive. You can tell them they will. You've been through it. Wasn't easy, but you survived. You and your spouse found dry land. Why don't you pluck an olive leaf and take it to an ark?

Are you a cancer survivor? Someone in the cancer ward needs to hear from you. Have you buried a spouse and lived to smile again? Then find the recently widowed and walk with them. Your experiences have deputized you into the dove brigade. You have an opportunity—yea, verily an obligation—to give hope to the arkbound.

Remember Paul's admonition?

> What a wonderful God we have—he is the Father of our Lord Jesus
> Christ, the source of every mercy, and the one who so wonderfully

comforts and strengthens us in our hardships and trials. And why does he do this? So that when others are troubled, needing our sympathy and encouragement, we can pass on to them this same help and comfort God has given us. (2 Cor. 1:3–4 TLB)

Encourage those who are struggling. Don't know what to say? Then open your Bible. The olive leaf for the Christian is a verse of Scripture. "For everything that was written in the past was written to teach us, so that through endurance and the encouragement of the Scriptures we might have hope" (Rom. 15:4 NIV).

Do you have a Bible? Do you know a Noah? Then start passing out the leaves.

To the grief stricken: "God has said, 'Never will I leave you; never will I forsake you'" (Heb. 13:5 NIV).

To the guilt ridden: "There is now no condemnation for those who are in Christ Jesus" (Rom. 8:1 NIV).

To the jobless: "In all things God works for the good of those who love him" (Rom. 8:28 NIV).

To those who feel beyond God's grace: "Whoever believes in him shall not perish but have eternal life" (John 3:16 NIV).

Your Bible is a basket of leaves. Won't you share one? They have amazing impact. After receiving his, Noah was a changed man. "Then Noah knew that the water had receded from the earth" (Gen. 8:11 NIV). He went up the ladder with questions and came down the ladder with confidence.

What a difference one leaf makes.

He Could Have
Given Up

Love . . . endures all things.

1 Corinthians 13:4–7 nasb

At any step along the way he could have called it quits. . . .

When he saw the dirt floor of his Nazareth house.

When Joseph gave him a chore to do.

When his fellow students were dozing off during the reading of the Torah, his Torah.

When the neighbor took his name in vain.

When the lazy farmer blamed his poor crop on God.

At any point Jesus could have said, "That's it! That's enough! I'm going home." But he didn't.

He didn't, because he is love.

He could have given up. No one would have known otherwise. Jesus could have given up.

One look at the womb could have discouraged him. God is as unbridled as the air and limitless as the sky. Would he reduce his world to the belly of a girl for nine months?

And nine months? There is another reason to quit. Heaven has no months. Heaven has no time. Or, perhaps better said, heaven has all the time. It's we who are running out. Ours passes so quickly that we measure it by the second. Wouldn't Christ rather stay on the other side of the ridge of time?

He could have. He could have given up. If not, at least he could have stopped short. Did he have to become *flesh*? How about becoming light? Here is an idea. Heaven could open, and Christ could fall on the earth in the form of a white light. And then in the light there could be a voice, a booming, thundering, teeth-shaking voice. Toss in a gust of wind and the angels for background vocals, and the whole world notices!

As things turned out, when he came, hardly anyone noticed. Bethlehem held no parade. The village offered no banquet. You'd think a holiday would have been appropriate. At least a few streamers for the stable.

And the stable. Is that not yet another reason for Christ to back out? Stables are smelly, dirty. Stables have no linoleum floors or oxygen tanks. How are they going to cut the umbilical cord? And who is going to cut the umbilical cord? Joseph? A small-time carpenter from a one-camel town? Is there not a better father for God? Someone with an education, a pedigree. Someone with a bit of clout? This fellow couldn't even swing a room at the hotel. You think he's got what it takes to be the father to the Maker of the universe?

Jesus could have given up. Imagine the change he had to make, the distance he had to travel. What would it be like to become flesh?

This question surfaced as I was golfing recently. Waiting my turn to putt, I squatted down to clean my ball and noticed a mountain of ants beside it. Must have been dozens of them, all over each other. A pyramid of motion at least half an inch tall.

I don't know what you think when you see ants on a green as you are waiting to putt. But here is what I thought: *Why are you guys all bunched up? You have the whole green. Why, the entire golf course is yours to spread out in.* Then it occurred to me. These ants are nervous. Who could blame them? They live under a constant meteor shower. Every few minutes a dimpled orb comes crashing into their world. *Bam! Bam! Bam!* Just when the bombing stops, the mallet-swinging giants arrive. If you survive their feet and sticks, they roll a meteor at you. A golf green is no place for an ant.

So I tried to help them. Leaning down where they could hear me, I invited, "Come on, follow me. We'll find a nice spot in the rough. I know it well." Not one looked in my direction. "Hey, ants!" Still no reply. Then I realized, *I don't speak their language.* I don't speak Ant. Pretty fluent in the idiom of Uncle, but I don't speak Ant.

So what could I do to reach them? Only one thing. I needed to become an ant. Go from six feet two inches to teeny-weeny. From 200-plus pounds to tenths of an ounce. Swap my big world for their tiny one. Give up burgers and start eating grass. "No thanks," I said. Besides, it was my turn to putt.

Love goes the distance . . . and Christ traveled from limitless eternity to be confined by time in order to become one of us. He didn't have to. He could have given up. At any step along the way he could have called it quits.

When he saw the size of the womb, he could have stopped.

When he saw how tiny his hand would be, how soft his voice would be, how hungry his tummy would be, he could have stopped. At the first whiff of the stinky stable, at the first gust of cold air. The first time he scraped his knee or blew his nose or tasted burnt bagels, he could have turned and walked out.

When he saw the dirt floor of his Nazareth house. When Joseph gave him a chore to do. When his fellow students were dozing off during the reading of the Torah, his Torah. When the neighbor took his name in vain. When the lazy farmer blamed his poor crop on God. At any point Jesus could have said, "That's it! That's enough! I'm going home." But he didn't.

He didn't, because he is love. And "love . . . endures all things" (1 Cor. 13:4–7 NKJV). He endured the distance. What's more, he endured the resistance.

"The Word became flesh and made his dwelling among us. We have seen his glory" (John 1:14 NIV).

"We have seen his glory." What did John mean by those words? Could it be that he saw in Christ flashes of heaven? Occasional, yet unforgettable, gasoline-on-the-fire flashes. Could it be that Christ would occasionally open his cape of humanity and allow a ray of glory to spill forth?

One of the regular attendees of our congregation is David Robinson. David is a big man. He stands seven feet two inches and weighs 235 pounds. His body fat is 6 percent. (I have that much in one thigh.) He is an NBA MVP, an NBA champion, and an NBA All-Star. But David is much more. He is a lover of God and a lover of kids. For that reason, the following scene won't be hard to imagine.

Let's say big-hearted David agrees to a game of one-on-one with a six-year-old girl. Just for the fun of it. She asks. He agrees. The two are on the same court, playing with the same ball, playing the same game, but everyone knows this isn't the same David. This is a mild David. A restrained David. A reserved David. How he plays against Shaq and how he plays against the girl are not the same.

Suppose some bully starts making fun of the little girl. He even comes out of the stands and taunts her. Calls her names and steals the ball from her. He throws it back so hard she falls over. You know what David might do? David might be David for a few moments. He might just take the dare and take the bully and dunk him like a donut.

For just a moment, the real David might take over.[1]

There were moments when the real Jesus did. Most of the time he was restrained. But then there were moments when he opened the cape. There were moments when he had all he could take of the bully from hell.

When the storm scared his followers, he stood and opened the cape: "Be still!" When death broke the hearts of his friends, he stepped into the cemetery and opened the cape: "Come forth!" When disease stole the joy of his children, he touched the leper with power: "Be healed!"

"For a moment"—John must have sighed when he wrote the words—"we beheld his glory."

A few, like John, were stunned by the sight. Others, however, missed it. They missed the glory of God. For whatever reason, they missed it. How did they react to his presence?

"They laughed at him" (Matt. 9:24 NIV).

"Many of them said, 'He is demon-possessed and raving mad. Why listen to him?'" (John 10:20 NIV).

They "hurled insults at him, shaking their heads" (Mark 15:29 NIV).

"The Pharisees, who loved money, heard all this and were sneering at Jesus" (Luke 16:14 NIV).

Isaiah prophesied the reception like this: "He was despised and rejected by men" (Isa. 53:3 NIV).

John summarized the rejection with these words: "He was in the world, and though the world was made through him, the world did not recognize him. He came to that which was his own, but his own did not receive him" (John 1:10–11 NIV).

How did Christ endure treatment like that? At any point he could have said, "I quit. I've had enough." Why didn't he? What kept him from giving up?

I wonder if Lee Ielpi understands the answer. He is a retired firefighter, a New York City firefighter. He gave twenty-six years to the city. But on September 11, 2001, he gave much more. He gave his son. Jonathan Ielpi was a fireman as well. When the Twin Towers fell, he was there.

Firefighters are a loyal clan. When one perishes in the line of duty, the body is left where it is until a firefighter who knows the person can come and quite literally pick it up. Lee made the discovery of his son's body his personal mission. He dug daily with dozens of others at the sixteen-acre graveyard. On Tuesday, December 11, three months after the disaster, his son was found. And Lee was there to carry him out.[2]

He didn't give up. The father didn't quit. He refused to turn and leave. Why? Because his love for his son was greater than the pain of the search. Can't the same be said about Christ? Why didn't he quit? Because the love for his children was greater than the pain of the journey. He came to pull you out. Your world had collapsed. That's why he came. You were dead, dead in sin. That's why he came. He loves you. That's why he came.

That's why he endured the distance between us. "Love . . . endures *all things.*"

That's why he endured the resistance from us. "Love . . . endures *all things*."

That's why he went the final step of the incarnation: "God made him who had no sin to be sin for us, so that in him we might become the right-eousness of God" (2 Cor. 5:21 NIV).

Why did Jesus do that? There is only one answer. And that answer has one word. Love. And the love of Christ "bears all things, believes all things, hopes all things, endures all things" (1 Cor. 13:7 NKJV).

Think about that for a moment. Drink from that for a moment. Drink deeply. Don't just sip or nip. It's time to gulp. It's time to let his love cover all things in your life. All secrets. All hurts. All hours of evil, minutes of worry.

The mornings you awoke in the bed of a stranger? His love will cover that. The years you peddled prejudice and pride? His love will cover that. Every promise broken, drug taken, penny stolen. Every cross word, cuss word, and harsh word. His love covers all things.

Let it. Discover along with the psalmist: "He . . . loads me with love and mercy" (Ps. 103:4). Picture a giant dump truck full of love. There you are behind it. God lifts the bed until the love starts to slide. Slowly at first, then down, down, down until you are hidden, buried, covered in his love.

"Hey, where are you?" someone asks.

"In here, covered in love."

Let his love cover all things.

Do it for his sake. To the glory of his name.

Do it for your sake. For the peace of your heart.

And do it for their sake. For the people in your life. Let his love fall on you so yours can fall on them.

CHAPTER SIXTEEN

UNFAILING LOVE

Love never fails.

1 CORINTHIANS 13:8 NIV

GOD LOVES YOU SIMPLY BECAUSE HE HAS CHOSEN TO DO SO.

HE LOVES YOU WHEN YOU DON'T FEEL LOVELY.

HE LOVES YOU WHEN NO ONE ELSE LOVES YOU.

OTHERS MAY ABANDON YOU, DIVORCE YOU, AND IGNORE YOU,

BUT GOD WILL LOVE YOU.

ALWAYS.

NO MATTER WHAT.

My friend Mike tells how his three-year-old daughter, Rachel, lost her balance and hit her head against the corner of an electric space heater. After a short cry, she blacked out. Her parents rushed her to the hospital, where the tests revealed a skull fracture.

Pretty traumatic for a child. Pretty traumatic for Mom and Dad. Rachel was kept overnight for observation and then sent home. She spent a couple of days understandably quiet. But Mike knew she was okay the morning he heard her talking to herself. He was still in bed, and she was down the hall in her room. "Bear? Doggie? Sheep? Baby? Ruff-ruff?" Mike smiled. She was calling roll in her crib, making sure her friends were all present. After all, she'd been through quite an ordeal, and she wanted to make sure things were in order.

A few moments of silence passed before she continued. "Eyes? Nose? Hair? Hand? Piggy?" Having verified the presence of her friends, Rachel was now taking inventory of herself.

Suppose we follow her lead? Before bringing this book to a close, let's take inventory. Let's take stock of our relationships. Think for a moment about the people in your world. If you want to write a few names in the margin, go ahead. Your husband, wife, kids, teachers, friends, parents, carpool buddies, coworkers. Give it some thought. Who populates your circle of the world?

As names surface, let me whisper a reminder. Aren't they valuable? Aren't they essential? Aren't those relationships worth whatever it takes to keep them healthy? Granted, people can be difficult. But still, what's more important than people?

Think of it this way. When you are in the final days of your life, what will you want? When death extends its hands to you, where will you turn for comfort? Will you hug that college degree in the walnut frame? Will you ask to be carried to the garage so you can sit in your car? Will you find comfort in rereading your financial statement? Of course not. What will matter then will be people. If relationships will matter most then, shouldn't they matter most now?

So what can you do to strengthen them? Following Rachel's example would be a good start. She inventoried her hands and hair; let's take inventory of our hearts. Am I living in the overflow of God's love? How well do I love the people in my life? Does the way I treat people reflect the way God has treated me?

Loving people isn't always easy. In fact, this book has been a challenging one for some of you. You've been forced to think again about some of the people in your life whom you find hard to love. This is serious business. It's not easy to love those who have been the source of heartache, abuse, rejection, or loneliness. Some of you wonder how you could ever love the people who have caused you such pain. So what can you do?

Conventional wisdom says that a lack of love implies a lack of effort, so we try harder, dig deeper, strain more.

But could a lack of love imply something else? Could we be skipping a step? An essential step? Could it be that we are trying to give what we don't have? Are we forgetting to receive first?

The woman in Capernaum didn't forget. Remember her from the first chapter? Remember how she lavished love on Christ? Bathing his feet with tears. Drying his feet with her hair. If love were a waterfall, she'd be a Niagara.

And Simon, well, Simon was a Sahara. Dry. Parched. Hard. His arid heart surprises us. He was the churchgoer, the pastor, the seminarian. She, on the other hand, was the town slut. He'd forgotten more Bible than she ever knew. But she'd discovered one truth Simon had somehow missed: God's love has no limits.

God's love meets the standard of our final passage. "Love," Paul says, "never fails" (1 Cor. 13:8 NIV).

The verb Paul uses for the word *fail* is used elsewhere to describe the demise of a flower as it falls to the ground, withers, and decays. It carries the meaning of death and abolishment. God's love, says the apostle, will never fall to the ground, wither, and decay. By its nature, it is permanent. It is never abolished.

Love "will last forever" (NLT).

It "never dies" (MSG).

It "never ends" (RSV).

Love "is eternal" (TEV).

God's love "will never come to an end" (NEB).

Love never fails.

Governments will fail, but God's love will last. Crowns are temporary, but love is eternal. Your money will run out, but his love never will.

How could God have a love like this? No one has unfailing love. No person can love with perfection. You're right. No person can. But God is not a person. Unlike our love, his never fails. His love is immensely different from ours.

Our love depends on the receiver of the love. Let a thousand people pass before us, and we will not feel the same about each. Our love will be regulated by their appearance, by their personalities. Even when we find a few people we like, our feelings will fluctuate. How they treat us will affect how we love them. The receiver regulates our love.

Not so with the love of God. We have no thermostatic impact on his love for us. The love of God is born from within him, not from what he finds in us. His love is uncaused and spontaneous. As Charles Wesley said, "He hath loved us. He hath loved us. Because he would love."[1]

Does he love us because of our goodness? Because of our kindness? Because of our great faith? No, he loves us because of *his* goodness, kindness, and great faith. John says it like this: "This is love: not that we loved God, but that he loved us" (1 John 4:10 NIV).

Doesn't this thought comfort you? God's love does not hinge on yours. The abundance of your love does not increase his. The lack of your love does not diminish his. Your goodness does not enhance his love, nor does your weakness dilute it. What Moses said to Israel is what God says to us:

> The LORD did not choose you and lavish his love on you because you were larger or greater than other nations, for you were the smallest of all nations! It was simply because the LORD loves you. (Deut. 7:7–8 NLT)

God loves you simply because he has chosen to do so.

He loves you when you don't feel lovely.

He loves you when no one else loves you. Others may abandon you, divorce you, and ignore you, but God will love you. Always. No matter what.

This is his sentiment: "I'll call nobodies and make them somebodies; I'll call the unloved and make them beloved" (Rom. 9:25 MSG).

This is his promise. "I have loved you, my people, with an everlasting love. With unfailing love I have drawn you to myself" (Jer. 31:3 NLT).

Do you know what else that means? You have a deep aquifer of love from which to draw. When you find it hard to love, then you need a drink! Drink deeply! Drink daily!

Don't forget, love is a fruit. Step into the orchard of God's work, and what is the first fruit you see? "*Love,* joy, peace, patience, kindness, goodness, faithfulness, gentleness and self-control" (Gal. 5:22 NIV, emphasis mine).

Love is a fruit. A fruit of whom? Of your hard work? Of your deep faith? Of your rigorous resolve? No. Love is a fruit of the Spirit of God. "The Spirit produces the fruit" (Gal. 5:22).

And, this is so important, you are a branch on the vine of God. "I am the vine, and you are the branches" (John 15:5). Need a refresher course on how vines function? What is the role of the branch in the bearing of fruit? Branches don't exert a lot of energy. You never hear of gardeners treating branches for exhaustion. Branches don't attend clinics on stress management. Nor do they groan and grunt: "I've got to get this grape out. I've got to get this grape out. I'm going to bear this grape if it kills me!"

No, the branch does none of that. The branch has one job—to receive nourishment from the vine. And you have one job—to receive nourishment from Jesus. "I am the Vine, you are the branches. When you're joined with me and I with you, the relation intimate and organic, the harvest is sure to be abundant. Separated, you can't produce a thing" (John 15:5 MSG).

Our Lord gets no argument from us on that last line, does he? We have learned the hard way—apart from him we can't produce a thing. Don't you think it's time we learn what happens if we stay attached?

His job is to bear fruit. Our job is to stay put. The more tightly we are attached to Jesus, the more purely his love can pass through us. And oh, what a love it is! Patient. Kind. Does not envy. Does not boast. Is not proud.

Let's rewrite 1 Corinthians 13:4–8 one more time. Not with your name or Jesus' name but with both. Read it aloud with your name in the blank, and see what you think.

> Christ in _____ is patient, Christ in _____ is kind. Christ in _____ does not envy, Christ in _____ does not boast, Christ in _____ is not proud. Christ in _____ is not rude, Christ in _____ is not self-seeking, Christ in _____ is not easily angered, Christ in _____ keeps no record of wrongs. Christ in _____ does not delight in evil but rejoices with the truth. Christ in _____ always protects, always trusts, always hopes, always perseveres. Christ in _____ never fails.

Will we ever love like that? Will we ever love perfectly? No. This side of heaven only God will. But we will love better than we have.

When kindness comes grudgingly, we'll remember his kindness to us and ask him to make us more kind. When patience is scarce, we'll thank him for his and ask him to make us more patient. When it's hard to forgive, we won't list all the times we've been given grief. Rather, we'll list all the times we've been given grace and pray to become more forgiving. We will receive first so we can give later. We will drink deeply from heaven's endless love. And when we do, we will discover a love worth giving.

DISCUSSION GUIDE

A LOVE WORTH GIVING

BY STEVE HALLIDAY

CHAPTER ONE

The 7:47 Principle

Love Remembered

1. We can't give what we've never received. If we've never received love, how can we love others?

    A. Do you agree that we can't give what we haven't received? Explain.

    B. How does someone "receive" love? How does someone "refuse" love?

    C. Have you received God's love? Explain.

2. Our relationships need more than a social gesture. Some of our spouses need a foot washing. A few of our friends need a flood of tears. Our children need to be covered in the oil of our love.

    A. If you are married, what does your spouse need today? What does your closest friend need? If you have children, what do they need?

    B. How can you cover others "in the oil" of your love?

    C. How do you need to be covered "in the oil" of others' love?

3. How can we love as God loves? We want to. We long to. But how can we? By living loved. By following the 7:47 Principle: Receive first, love second.

    A. How does God love *you?*

    B. What does the phrase "living loved" mean to you? Are you living loved? Explain.

    C. How do you receive God's love on a day-to-day basis?

Love Deepened

1. Read Luke 7:36–50.

   A. In your own words, describe the scene depicted here. What happened?

   B. What lesson did Jesus want Simon to learn? How did he communicate this lesson?

   C. What principle did Jesus develop in verse 47? How does this principle relate to you? Explain.

2. Read 1 John 4:9–11.

   A. What does God's love look like?

   B. How is our love supposed to take its cue from God?

   C. Why did God love us? Why are we supposed to love others?

3. Read Ephesians 4:32–5:2.

   A. What three commands does God give us in verse 32? What example does he provide to show *how* we are to obey these commands?

   B. What command does God give us in verse 1? In what way can we obey this command? What gives us the ability to obey this command, according to the second part of the verse?

   C. What command does God give us in verse 2? What example are we given? How can we practically follow this example?

Love Given

1. Think of the person closest to you (whether spouse, friend, child, parent, etc.). Periodically throughout one entire day, take a little notepad, and list the reasons why this person is so close to you. Why do you love him or her? Then at the end of the day, make another list

by responding to the question "How can I do a better job of showing love to this person?" Last, before the end of the week, begin doing at least one of the things you wrote on the second list.

2. What volunteer opportunities are available in your neighborhood or city? Carve out some time in the next month to serve others in an arena unfamiliar to you. How can you show these people the love of God?

CHAPTER TWO

LOVE'S FLAGSHIP

Love Remembered

1. Paul presents patience as the premiere expression of love. Positioned at the head of the apostle's Love Armada—a boat-length or two in front of kindness, courtesy, and forgiveness—is the flagship known as patience.

   A. Have you ever thought of patience as "the premiere expression of love"? Explain.

   B. Why do you think Paul positioned patience at the head of his Love Armada? What is it about patience that best shows love?

   C. Do you consider yourself a patient person? Explain.

   D. How does God try to build your patience?

2. Patience is more than a virtue for long lines and slow waiters. Patience is the red carpet upon which God's grace approaches us.

   A. In what way is patience the red carpet upon which God's grace approaches us?

   B. How is God patient with us? How is God patient with *you*?

   C. How are grace and patience related? How do they play off of one another?

3. How infiltrated are you with God's patience? You've heard about it. Read about it. Perhaps underlined Bible passages regarding it. But have you received it? The proof is in your patience.

A. What does it mean to "receive" God's patience? Have you received it? Explain.

B. Thus far in your life, what have you learned in God's Word about patience? Do you struggle with any of these lessons? Explain.

C. Would others say that you are a patient person? Explain.

Love Deepened

1. Read Romans 2:1–4.

    A. How does a tendency to judge others reveal a lack of understanding about God's patience? Do you struggle with judging others? Explain.

    B. How is it possible to show contempt for the riches of God's kindness (v. 4)?

    C. How does God's patience lead us toward repentance?

    D. Where would you be if God were not patient with you? Why is it important to remember this when you deal with others?

2. Read 2 Peter 3:8–9.

    A. What does Peter want to make sure we don't forget (v. 8)? Why is this so important?

    B. Why do we sometimes think the Lord is slow in keeping his promise?

    C. Why is God patient with us (v. 9)? What is his motivation?

    D. How can we model God's patience in dealing with others?

3. Read Matthew 18:21–35.

    A. What prompted Jesus to tell this story? What do you think was behind the question to Jesus?

    B. Retell the story in your own words.

C. What was the first servant's problem? What was the second servant's problem?

D. What is the main point of Jesus' story? How does it affect you? Explain.

E. How does Jesus' story answer Peter's question in verse 21? How does this relate to patience?

Love Given

1. Sit down with a sheet of paper and a pen or pencil, and write out your answers to the following questions: How has God shown you patience in the past week? How has he shown you patience in the past year? Did he show patience in bringing you to salvation? If so, how? How have you responded to his patience?

2. With whom are you most likely to display impatience? A spouse? A son or a daughter? A coworker? A neighbor? Spend some protracted time this week praying about your impatience toward this person. Ask God to show you specifically what you can do to show patience to this person. Then monitor your behavior over the next month, and invite God to encourage and discipline you as needed.

CHAPTER THREE

YOUR KINDNESS QUOTIENT

Love Remembered

1. The kindness of Jesus. We are quick to think of his power, his passion, and his devotion. But those near him knew and know God comes cloaked in kindness.

   A. Do you usually think of kindness when you ponder Jesus? Explain.

   B. What does kindness mean to you? How have people shown you kindness?

   C. What does it mean to be "cloaked" in kindness? What does this image suggest to you?

2. Isn't kindness good *and* good for you? Pleasant *and* practical? Kindness not only says good morning, kindness makes the coffee.

   A. How has the kindness of others ministered to you?

   B. How is kindness both pleasant and practical?

   C. Why can genuine kindness never be inactive? Why must it always be doing *something*?

3. How kind are you? What is your kindness quotient? When was the last time you did something kind for someone in your family—e.g., got a blanket, cleaned off the table, prepared the coffee—without being asked?

   A. How would you answer each of these questions?

B. Would others use the word *kind* to describe you? Explain, especially if they see you differently than you see yourself.

Love Deepened

1. Read Titus 3:3–7.

   A. How does Paul describe those who haven't yet received God's love (v. 3)?

   B. In what way did the kindness of God appear (v. 4)? What form did this kindness take?

   C. How does God's kindness connect to our salvation? What part did God's kindness play in his offer of salvation?

   D. What concrete images does Paul give us of God's kindness in this passage? What did God's kindness *do*?

2. Read Luke 6:27–36.

   A. List the various commands Jesus gives us in this passage.

   B. How does kindness relate to all of these commands?

   C. Why does Jesus tell us that God "is kind to the ungrateful and wicked" (v. 35 NIV)? What effect is that statement supposed to have upon us?

   D. In what way does Jesus connect God's kindness to the mercy we are to show others (vv. 34–35)?

3. Read Colossians 3:12–14.

   A. With what are we told to clothe ourselves?

   B. List the practical ways in which this passage fleshes out kindness. What does kindness do? What does it not do?

Love Given

1. Read through the Gospel of your choice, noting instances in which

Jesus did something kind. How did the Master show God's kindness? How can we imitate his work?

2. Jesus tells us to be kind even to those who mistreat us. Who in your sphere of influence has been unkind to you? What act of kindness could you show this person this week? Plan such an act, and then follow through with it. Pray that God will use it to touch this person, but even if the person doesn't respond in kind, determine that you will continue to reflect God's kindness regardless.

CHAPTER FOUR

INFLAMED

Love Remembered

1. What is born in innocence is deadly in adolescence. Left untended, fire consumes all that is consumable.

   A. What does envy look like in innocence? How is it deadly in adolescence?

   B. How does envy consume those it touches?

   C. In what situations are you most likely to struggle with envy? How do you deal with it?

2. God withholds what we desire in order to give us what we need.

   A. What desires has God so far withheld from you? Why do you think he has done so?

   B. Describe a time when God withheld a personal desire in order to meet a personal need.

   C. What do you think you most need today? Explain.

3. Your Father . . . offers authentic love. His devotion is the real deal. But he won't give you the genuine until you surrender the imitations.

   A. How would you describe God's authentic love, the "real deal"? How have you experienced it?

   B. What imitations have you held on to in the past?

   C. How can you surrender the imitations? What does this entail?

Love Deepened

1. Read Psalm 37:1–3.

   A. Why are we tempted to fret because of evil men and to grow envious because of those who do wrong?

   B. In this passage how does David suggest we fight envy? Of what are we to remind ourselves?

   C. In what way is trust an antidote to envy?

2. Read Proverbs 14:30.

   A. Describe a heart at peace. What does it look like? How does such a heart give "life to the body"?

   B. How does envy "rot the bones"? What does this mean?

   C. How does one get a heart at peace and avoid envy-rotted bones?

3. Read James 4:1–6.

   A. According to James, what causes fights and quarrels among us (v. 1)?

   B. Describe a time you witnessed the destructive power of envy in a relationship.

   C. What is the antidote to envy and the quarrels it produces?

   D. James says the Spirit envies intensely (v. 5)—and this is a good thing. In what sense does he envy? How can this kind of divine envy be good but our kind of envy be bad?

Love Given

1. Try to come at envy from another direction. What things do you have (talents, resources, possessions, relationships) that others might envy? Be as honest as possible: Have you ever flaunted these things to inflame the envy of others? If so, what can you do to lessen the possibility that you might make others envious?

CHAPTER FIVE

GOD'S "NO PECKING" ZONE

Love Remembered

1. Would you do what Jesus did? He swapped a spotless castle for a grimy stable. He exchanged the worship of angels for the company of killers. He could hold the universe in his palm but gave it up to float in the womb of a maiden.

   A. Answer the previous question, then explain your answer.

   B. What do you think was hardest for Jesus to give up? Why?

   C. If you had been Jesus, what do you think you would have done differently? Explain.

2. What's more important to you—that the work be done or that you be seen? When a brother or sister is honored, are you joyful or jealous?

   A. Answer the previous questions. Why did you answer as you did?

   B. Describe the last time you did an excellent job but kept completely silent about it.

   C. Would you consider yourself a humble person? Explain.

3. True humility is not thinking lowly of yourself but thinking accurately of yourself. The humble heart does not say, "I can't do anything." But rather, "I can't do everything. I know my part and am happy to do it."

   A. Do you know your strengths as well as your weaknesses? Explain.

   B. Are you happy to do your part? Explain.

C. Who is the most humble person you know? Describe him or her. What makes him or her so humble?

Love Deepened

1. Read Matthew 23:5–12.

   A. How do verses 5–7 paint a picture of showboating? What's so wrong with this picture?

   B. How does Jesus tell us to combat such showboating (vv. 8–11)?

   C. How can a servant be great?

   D. What does Jesus promise to do for the humble? What does he promise to do for those who exalt themselves (v. 12)?

2. Read Philippians 2:3–11.

   A. What general principle does Paul give us in verse 3? How is this principle to be lived out practically?

   B. How does verse 4 give us a practical way to show humility? How could you put this into practice to a greater degree in your own life?

   C. How did Jesus exemplify a lifestyle of humility?

   D. How will God reward Jesus for his humility? In what way does this provide an incentive for us?

3. Read Romans 12:3–10.

   A. How are we to think of ourselves (v. 3)? What does this mean?

   B. How does remembering the Christian body help us to remain humble (vv. 4–8)?

   C. How are we to honor one another above ourselves (v. 10)? What might this entail for you personally?

Love Given

1. Plan an "Honor Day." Give your time to someone else: an older person, a child, an invalid. Demonstrate Christlike love to that person by helping him or her feel special. At the end of the day, journal all you've learned about serving and loving.

2. Hold a little foot-washing ceremony. Go to a relative or friend, read John 13:1–17 aloud, and then reenact the scene. And be sure your servanthood stays with you beyond the reenactment!

CHAPTER SIX

A CALL TO COMMON COURTESY

Love Remembered

1. When defining what love is not, Paul put rudeness on the list.

   A. What's the rudest thing anyone has ever done to you?

   B. Describe the rudest thing you've ever done to someone else.

   C. How do you feel when someone is rude to you? How do you usually respond?

2. God calls us to a higher, more noble concern. Not "What are my rights?" but "What is loving?"

   A. Be honest: Do you usually think first about your rights or about what is most loving?

   B. What does courtesy have to do with love?

   C. Describe the most loving thing you did this week.

3. Does not the groom cherish the bride? Respect the bride? Honor the bride? Let Christ do what he longs to do. For as you receive his love, you'll find it easier to give yours.

   A. Why are a bride and groom almost never rude to one another during the wedding ceremony? What changes in the marriage?

   B. In what environments are you most tempted to be rude? How can you overcome the temptation?

Love Deepened

1. Read Luke 4:22.

   A. Why did everyone (at first) speak well of Jesus?

   B. What kind of words came from Jesus' lips?

   C. How are such words the opposite of rude?

2. Read Colossians 4:6.

   A. How can our conversation be full of grace?

   B. What does it mean to "season" our words "with salt"?

   C. What is the purpose of this grace and seasoning in our speech?

3. Read Romans 12:16.

   A. What does "living in harmony" say about God's people?

   B. What is the relationship between pride and rudeness?

   C. Why should we be willing to associate with people of low position?

   D. How can we keep from becoming conceited?

Love Given

1. Sit down with a loved one, and watch a favorite movie. Watch especially for scenes where someone is rude. What happened in the story because of the rude behavior? What might have happened had the behavior not occurred? How would a humble spirit have changed things?

2. All of us will, at some point, be subjected to rude behavior. Be proactive and think ahead of time how you will react to it. What stock phrases might you use to defuse the situation? How can you prepare yourself to infuse the incident with God's grace?

CHAPTER SEVEN

Getting the "I" Out of Your Eye

Love Remembered

1. Selfishness is an obsession with self that excludes others, hurting everyone.

   A. How would you describe selfishness?

   B. Describe a time when someone's selfishness hurt you badly.

   C. Describe a time when your selfishness hurt someone else.

2. Desire success? Fine. Just don't hurt others in achieving it. Wish to look nice? That's okay. Just don't do so by making others look bad.

   A. How do we sometimes hurt others in trying to achieve success? How is this selfish?

   B. How do we try to make ourselves look nice by making others look bad?

   C. How would you respond to someone who said, "Well, if I don't take care of myself, who will?"

3. What's the cure for selfishness? Get your self out of your eye by getting your eye off your self. Quit staring at that little self, and focus on your great Savior.

   A. What do you think of this cure for selfishness?

   B. How can one put this cure into action, practically speaking? How can it become more than a nice set of words?

Love Deepened

1. Read James 3:13–16.

   A. How would James define "selfish ambition"?

   B. What does it accomplish? To what does it lead? From where does it come?

   C. How can we combat selfish ambition?

2. Read Psalm 119:36.

   A. What prayer does the psalmist offer in this verse?

   B. How can God's Word help to turn us away from selfish gain?

   C. How do you use the Bible to combat selfishness?

3. Read Romans 2:7–8.

   A. To what group of people will God give eternal life (v. 7)?

   B. What awaits those who are self-seeking (v. 8)?

   C. Why is there such a difference between these two groups?

Love Given

1. In what area of life are you tempted to be most selfish? Since selfishness never goes away by itself, you need to put together a plan to kill it. How can you most effectively confront your self-seeking tendencies? Think about this on your own, then discuss your plan with the person closest to you. Together try to put your plan into action.

2. A good way to combat selfishness is to get into the habit of giving to others. Rather than giving something you don't need or use, select something personal and meaningful to share with someone who is lonely or overlooked.

CHAPTER EIGHT

THE HEADWATERS OF ANGER .

Love Remembered

1. The fire of anger has many logs, but according to biblical accounts, the thickest and the hottest block of wood is rejection.

   A. What makes you angry?

   B. Does rejection make you angry? Explain.

   C. Why does rejection anger most of us?

2. If rejection causes anger, wouldn't acceptance cure it? If rejection by heaven makes you mad at others, wouldn't acceptance from heaven stir your love for them?

   A. Does acceptance always cure anger? Explain.

   B. How does heaven's acceptance prompt us to show love toward others?

   C. If this statement is true, then why do many Christians seem to be so angry? Why are many believers lacking in love?

3. Rejections are like speed bumps on the road. They come with the journey. . . . You cannot keep people from rejecting you. But you can keep rejections from enraging you.

   A. Can we keep rejections from injuring us? Explain.

   B. How can we keep rejections from enraging us?

   C. How have you learned to best deal with rejection?

Love Deepened

1. Read Genesis 4:2–8.

   A. What caused Cain's anger in this account?

   B. How did God respond to Cain's anger (vv. 6–7)?

   C. How did Cain deal with his anger (v. 8)?

   D. What can we learn from Cain about how *not* to deal with anger?

2. Read Romans 9:1–5.

   A. How did Paul feel toward his countrymen? Why did he feel this way?

   B. Paul had great cause to oppose his Jewish brothers, but he didn't. Why not?

   C. Upon what did Paul focus in order to maintain his love for his estranged brothers and sisters (v. 5)? How can we follow his example?

3. Read John 5:6.

   A. What question did Jesus ask of the invalid?

   B. Why would Jesus ask the man such a question? Wouldn't the answer be obvious?

   C. If Jesus were to ask you this question regarding your anger, what would you say? Explain.

Love Given

1. Make a detailed study of Ephesians 4:26. Read this verse in several translations, research what commentators say about it, and meditate on it in your quiet times for several weeks. At the end of your study, try to bring to life what you've learned. What can you do in your home to better comply with God's command? What can you do at work? In church? In your neighborhood?

CHAPTER NINE

THE HEART FULL OF HURTS

Love Remembered

1. Our assignment is to protect the boat and refuse entrance to trashy thoughts. The minute they appear on the dock we go into action. "This heart belongs to God," we declare, "and you aren't getting on board until you change your allegiance."

    A. How vigilant have you been in refusing entrance to trashy thoughts?

    B. Describe some strategies that either you or your acquaintances have used to police the thought life.

    C. How can you get a wicked thought out of your mind once it's entered? Is it possible to drive it away? Explain.

2. You have not been sprinkled with forgiveness. You have not been spattered with grace. You have not been dusted with kindness. You have been immersed in it. You are submerged in mercy. You are a minnow in the ocean of his mercy.

    A. What does it mean to you to be immersed in God's grace?

    B. Why is it important to know that God has not merely sprinkled us with his goodness?

    C. Describe someone you know who thinks God is a miser with his kindness and mercy. How does this person move through life?

3. You can stick with your long lists and stinky cargo. And drift from port to port. But why would you? Let the *Pelicano* have the high seas. Your Captain has better plans for you.

   A. To what "long lists" and "stinky cargo" does Max refer?

   B. Why would anyone choose to stick with such loathsome cargo? Have you ever chosen to stick with it? Explain.

   C. What plans does your Captain have for you? How does your knowledge of these plans change the way you move through life?

Love Deepened

1. Read Colossians 2:13–15.

   A. What kind of "trash" does Paul speak of in this passage?

   B. How did Christ deal with it? What did he nail to the cross?

   C. How did Christ triumph through the cross? How can we share in this triumph?

2. Read 2 Corinthians 10:4–5.

   A. What kind of weapons does Paul have in mind here?

   B. What kind of strongholds does Paul have in mind here?

   C. How do these weapons demolish these strongholds?

3. Read Philippians 4:8.

   A. Paul lists several characteristics of the kinds of thoughts we are to entertain. Name them.

   B. How can we fill our minds with such thoughts?

   C. Why do we sometimes disobey this instruction?

Love Given

1. How can you help the members of your family to "take captive every

thought" to Christ (2 Cor. 10:5 NIV)? Do you allow any stumbling blocks to trip up your loved ones, whether they come in the form of trashy entertainment, inappropriate magazines, or other unhelpful media offerings? Do an inventory of your home. Physically walk through every room in the house, and ask yourself, "Is there anything in this room that better belongs on the *Pelicano*?"

CHAPTER TEN

THE LOVE TEST

Love Remembered

1. Feelings can fool you.
    A. Describe a time when your feelings fooled you.
    B. How do feelings fool us? How do they manage to deceive us?
    C. How does our culture encourage us to do whatever we feel? How can we resist its unwise urgings?

2. True love will never ask the "beloved" to do what he or she thinks is wrong. Love doesn't tear down the convictions of others. Quite the contrary.
    A. Describe a time when someone tried to use "love" to get you to do something you considered wrong. What happened?
    B. Why will genuine love never encourage someone to do something he or she considers wrong? What if the person's convictions are themselves wrong?
    C. How does true love attempt to persuade its beloved to take a certain course of action?

3. You want to plumb the depths of your love for someone? How do you feel when that person succeeds? Do you rejoice? Or are you jealous? And when he or she stumbles? Falls to misfortune? Are you really sorry? Or are you secretly pleased? Love never celebrates misfortune. Never.

A. Answer the previous questions, then explain your answers.

B. Why does love never celebrate misfortune?

C. How does love react to a *deserved* misfortune?

Love Deepened

1. Read 1 Corinthians 8:1–13.

   A. What relationship does Paul see between knowledge and love (vv. 1–3)? Which ought to take the lead? Why?

   B. How did love control Paul's use of his knowledge about idols (vv. 9–11)?

   C. What general principle does Paul develop out of this discussion (vv. 12–13)?

2. Read Luke 13:34–35.

   A. What truth did Jesus know about the future of Jerusalem?

   B. How did this truth affect him?

   C. Did Jesus rejoice over the judgment of his enemies? Why or why not?

3. Read Psalm 147:10–11.

   A. In what things does the Lord *not* take pleasure (v. 10)? Why not?

   B. In what *does* the Lord take pleasure (v. 11)? Why?

   C. What kind of love does the Lord express toward us? Why should this give us hope?

Love Given

1. Celebrate an unexpected success enjoyed by someone in your family. Make it fun, memorable, and significant. Make sure the person whose success you celebrate knows how much joy you take in him or her, not just because of the success, but because of who he or she is.

2. Take stock of how you react when a believing brother or sister enjoys some success. Can you truly rejoice with that person, or do you feel a little envious? Also consider how you react when a rival takes a stumble. Do you enjoy it? Ask the Lord to show you your heart, and then ask him to help you become more like Christ.

CHAPTER ELEVEN

LOVE IS A PACKAGE DEAL

Love Remembered

1. Wouldn't it be great if love were like a cafeteria line? It would be easier. It would be neater. It would be painless and peaceful. But you know what? It wouldn't be love. Love doesn't accept just a few things. Love is willing to accept all things.

   A. Have you ever known someone who treated love like a cafeteria line? If so, how did this person treat others?

   B. Does the fact that love is willing to accept all things mean that love never tries to change some of those things? Explain.

   C. What kinds of things in a loved one are hardest for you to accept? Explain.

2. God's view of love is like my mom's view of food. When we love someone, we take the entire package.

   A. Describe some of the ways we try *not* to take the entire package.

   B. What part of your entire package have others had a hard time accepting? Explain.

   C. How can we accept someone's whole person when there are parts of his or her personality that we dislike?

3. Jesus bore all things, believed all things, hoped all things, and endured all things. Every single one.

A. Why is it important for us to remember that Jesus himself endured all things? How can this knowledge change our behavior toward others?

B. What might have happened if Jesus had refused to endure all things? What would have happened to you?

C. How can we learn to imitate Jesus' example of enduring all things?

Love Deepened

1. Read 1 Corinthians 1:10–17.

   A. What church problem does Paul discuss in this passage? Is such a problem common today? Explain.

   B. How did Paul want the church to behave (v. 10)? Is such a hope realistic? Explain.

   C. What might have happened in Corinth had the church learned to bear all things among its membership? Explain.

2. Read 1 Corinthians 5:1–13.

   A. Does this passage fit with the idea that love bears all things? Explain.

   B. How does this passage illustrate the difference between the judgment of behavior and the judgment of motivation?

   C. How is it possible to love a brother or sister who sins and yet refuse to tolerate the sin? Why is this so hard to put into practice?

3. Read Romans 12:18.

   A. What command are we given in this verse?

   B. How does the idea of bearing all things help us to obey this command?

Love Given

1. Here's an exercise to try only if you're feeling pretty satisfied with yourself. Make a list of what you believe to be your most annoying habits or traits. Be brutally honest. As you think about this list, which habits or traits can you realistically do something about? How can you work on them to make it easier for those around you to bear all things?

2. Identify the person in your sphere of influence who you believe best exemplifies the loving trait of bearing all things. Make an appointment to interview this person. What can you learn that might help you to better bear all things?

CHAPTER TWELVE

A Cloak of Love

Love Remembered

1. The scholar sounds poetic as he explains the meaning of *protect* as used in 1 Corinthians 13:7. The word conveys, he says, "the idea of covering with a cloak of love."

    A. Describe someone you know who is good at covering with a cloak of love.

    B. Describe a time when someone covered you with a cloak of love.

    C. Try to come up with several other images that convey this idea of protecting in love. What pictures convey loving protection to you?

2. We hide. He seeks. We bring sin. He brings a sacrifice. We try fig leaves. He brings the robe of righteousness.

    A. How do we try to hide when we sin? How do *you* try to hide?

    B. What motivates God to bring a sacrifice for our sin?

    C. How does one put on a robe of righteousness? Have you put on such a robe? Explain.

3. Do you know anyone, like Madge, who is wounded and afraid? Do you know anyone, like Adam and Eve, who is guilty and embarrassed? Do you know anyone who needs a cloak of love?

    A. Answer the previous questions.

    B. How can you help those you identified to put on a cloak of love?

C. Who has been a protector for you? Describe the person.

Love Deepened

1. Read Matthew 25:31–46.

   A. What scene is depicted in verses 31–33?

   B. How does the king describe the blessed ones in verses 34–36? What had they done?

   C. Why are the blessed ones surprised at the king's statement (vv. 37–39)?

   D. How does the king respond to their surprise (v. 40)?

   E. What does this suggest to us about our responsibility to protect the less fortunate?

2. Read 2 Thessalonians 3:1–3.

   A. What request did Paul make of his Thessalonian friends (v. 1)? Why did he make this request?

   B. What additional request did Paul make (v. 2)? How does this prayer relate to protection?

   C. What promise does God make through the apostle in verse 3? Can we take advantage of this promise? Explain.

3. Read Matthew 14:22–33.

   A. Recount in your own words what happened in this story.

   B. In how many ways did Jesus protect his disciples in this incident?

   C. How can this story give us hope? What can we learn from it?

Love Given

1. Using a good concordance, do a word study on the term *protect,* along with related words such as *protects, protected,* and *protection.* What do

you learn about how God protects his children? What does this do for your sense of security? How can you use this knowledge to help others build their trust in God?

2. Matthew 25 makes it plain that Christ wants us to protect and help the less fortunate among us. What are *you* currently doing to feed the hungry, give drink to the thirsty, house the homeless, clothe the naked, care for the sick, and visit those in prison? If you want to take Christ's words seriously, what *can* you do?

CHAPTER THIRTEEN

THE RING OF BELIEF

Love Remembered

1. God believes in you. And, I wonder, could you take some of the belief that he has in you and share it with someone else? Could you believe in someone?

   A. Do you agree that God believes in you? Explain.

   B. How can we share God's belief in us with others?

   C. How has someone shown that he or she believed in you? What did this belief do for you?

2. Right or wrong, we define ourselves through other people's eyes. Tell me enough times that I'm stupid, and I'll believe you. Tell me enough times that I'm bright, and I might agree.

   A. Do you tend to define yourself through the eyes of others? Explain.

   B. Describe a time when someone's comments about you affected your self-image or behavior.

   C. How do you try to show people that you believe in them? What do you say to them?

3. How do we show people that we believe in them? *Show up. . . . Listen up. . . . Speak up.*

   A. How do you show up in the lives of others? How do they show up in yours?

B. How do you listen up in the lives of others? How do they listen up in yours?

C. How do you speak up in the lives of others? How do they speak up in yours?

Love Deepened

1. Read Luke 15:11–23.

    A. Describe the main characters in this story. What are they like?

    B. What is the main point of this story? What are we to take away from it?

    C. In what way is the father in the story a picture of God? How does God act like the father?

    D. How did the father show his belief in his son? How did this belief affect his son?

2. Read Proverbs 18:21; 12:18; 15:2, 4.

    A. What powers are attributed to the tongue in these verses?

    B. How does the tongue of the wise bring healing?

    C. How can you teach your own tongue to bring life and healing? What may have to change to make that happen?

3. Read Ephesians 4:29.

    A. What is prohibited in this verse?

    B. What is commended in this verse?

    C. What good result is described in this verse?

    D. Are you complying with this verse? Explain.

Love Given

1. Try your hand as an author. Write an account of how someone

showed his or her belief in you, including as many details as possible. Tell what he or she did, as well as what happened in your life as a result. Then share your story with a friend or loved one.

2. How can you show someone else that you believe in him or her? This week pick someone at home or in the office who needs to hear that you believe in him or her, and think of a creative way to express your belief. Send a card, make a call, arrange a lunch, plan a special outing—but don't let this week go by without expressing your belief in this individual.

CHAPTER FOURTEEN

When You're Low on Hope

Love Remembered

1. Hope is an olive leaf—evidence of dry land after a flood. Proof to the dreamer that dreaming is worth the risk.

    A. In what areas of your life do you most need hope right now?

    B. How has hope rescued you from a "flood" in the past?

    C. What dreams do you hold dear? Do you believe they are worth the risk? Explain.

2. With all due respect, our severest struggles are, in God's view, nothing worse than lost bobby pins and rubber bands. He is not confounded, confused, or discouraged. Receive his hope, won't you? Receive it because you need it. Receive it so you can share it.

    A. How big is your God? Can he handle your problems? Explain.

    B. How would you feel if God *could* be confused or discouraged?

    C. How do you receive God's hope? How can you share it?

3. Love extends an olive leaf to the loved one and says, "I have hope in you." Love is just as quick to say, "I have hope *for* you."

    A. What does it mean to say that love declares, "I have hope in you"?

    B. What does it mean to say that love declares, "I have hope *for* you"?

    C. How can you declare to those nearest to you that you have hope in them and for them? What do you think such a declaration would mean to them?

Love Deepened

1. Read Romans 8:18–25.
   A. Why did Paul not grumble about his present sufferings (v. 18)?
   B. To what did Paul look forward (vv. 19–21)? How did this expectation change his outlook?
   C. Did Paul downplay his troubles (vv. 22–23)? How did he forbid them from bringing him down?
   D. How did Paul understand hope (vv. 24–25)? How can his understanding help us in our difficult times?

2. Read Romans 15:4.
   A. Why was the Bible written, according to this verse?
   B. How do we receive hope, according to this verse?
   C. Why do we need hope?

3. Read Hebrews 13:5–6.
   A. Why can we be content with what we have (v. 5)?
   B. What promise does God make to us in this passage?
   C. How can this promise give us hope?
   D. How can this hope change the way we live (v. 6)?

Love Given

1. Read a good book on the topic of hope. How has God designed our faith to give us hope, even in trying times?

2. Pretend you're a journalist for a while, and do some investigative

reporting. Ask several of your coworkers or neighbors to talk about hope: whether they have it, what they think it is, how it changes things, where it comes from, etc. Is hope a common or a rare commodity these days? How can you give people hope?

CHAPTER FIFTEEN

HE COULD HAVE GIVEN UP

Love Remembered

1. Jesus could have given up.

   A. If you had been the devil, how would you have tempted Jesus to give up?

   B. Why do you think Jesus *didn't* give up? What kept him on track?

   C. What would have happened had Jesus given up? How would history have changed?

2. Love goes the distance . . . and Christ traveled from limitless eternity to be confined by time in order to become one of us.

   A. In what ways does love go the distance? How has it gone the distance in your own life?

   B. How did love cause Jesus to relocate from heaven to earth?

3. Why didn't he quit? Because the love for his children was greater than the pain of the journey. He came to pull you out. Your world had collapsed. That's why he came. You were dead, dead in sin. That's why he came.

   A. How did love overcome pain in Jesus' life? How can it do the same in your life?

   B. How did Jesus pull you out of your collapsed world?

   C. What does it mean to be dead in sin? How did Jesus' coming rescue us from sin and death?

Love Deepened

1. Read Hebrews 12:2–3.

   A. What guidance does the writer give us in verse 2? What is the reason for this guidance?

   B. How did Jesus endure the Cross, according to the writer? To what joy does he refer (v. 2)?

   C. In what way can we follow Jesus' example here (v. 3)? What happens when we do follow his example?

2. Read 2 Corinthians 4:7–18.

   A. Why does Paul call our bodies "jars of clay" (v. 7)? What is God's purpose in giving us such bodies?

   B. How does Paul describe his challenges and hardships (vv. 8–10)? How did he endure them?

   C. What hope drove Paul and gave him such endurance (v. 14)? Do you share this hope? Explain.

   D. What is one secret to not losing heart (v. 16)?

   E. What is the key to endurance (v. 18)? Have you found this key? Explain.

3. Read Revelation 1:9.

   A. What is "ours in Jesus," according to Revelation 1:9 (NIV)? Why is it ours?

   B. How might Colossians 1:3–12 give insight into John's statement?

Love Given

1. Read a good biography of a missionary, looking especially for the ways in which the missionary endured and persevered despite hardship. What can you learn for your own Christian life from this person's experience?

2. Be on the lookout this week for someone in your life who desperately needs encouragement. What can you do to help this person endure? Invite him or her to breakfast or lunch, and gently probe how you might offer hope and assistance.

CHAPTER SIXTEEN

UNFAILING LOVE

Love Remembered

1. When you are in the final days of your life, what will you want? When death extends its hands to you, where will you turn for comfort?

   A. Answer the previous questions.

   B. Describe someone in your life who exemplifies unfailing love. What is this person like?

2. Let's take inventory of our hearts. Am I living in the overflow of God's love? How well do I love the people in my life? Does the way I treat people reflect the way God has treated me?

   A. Answer the previous questions.

   B. How does one live in the overflow of God's love? What does this mean?

   C. List ten ways God has shown you his love. How have you passed on this love to others?

3. God's love does not hinge on yours. The abundance of your love does not increase his. The lack of your love does not diminish his. Your goodness does not enhance his love, nor does your weakness dilute it.

   A. Why does God's love not hinge on yours?

   B. How does it make you feel that God's love is unchanging?

   C. How do we know that God's love is unchanging?

4. Let's rewrite 1 Corinthians 13:4–8 one more time. Not with your name or Jesus' name but with both. Read it aloud with your name in the blank, and see what you think.

> Christ in _____ is patient, Christ in _____ is kind. Christ in ____ does not envy, Christ in _____ does not boast, Christ in ____ is not proud. Christ in _____ is not rude, Christ in ____ is not self-seeking, Christ in ____ is not easily angered, Christ in ____ keeps no record of wrongs. Christ in _____ does not delight in evil but rejoices with the truth. Christ in _____ always protects, always trusts, always hopes, always perseveres. Christ in _____ never fails.

A. How did this passage sound, with both your name and Christ's in it? Explain.

B. What changes does such a reading urge you to make in your Christian walk? Explain.

Love Deepened

1. Read Deuteronomy 7:7–9.
   A. What were *not* factors in God's setting his affection on Israel (v. 7)?
   B. Why *did* God set his affection on Israel (v. 8)?
   C. In what way is this principle the same for all believers in Christ today?

2. Read 1 Corinthians 13:8–13.
   A. Why will prophecies, tongues, and knowledge cease? Why will love never cease?
   B. To what day does Paul refer when he speaks of perfection coming (v. 10)? When will we see God "face to face" (v. 12)? When will we know fully, even as we are fully known (v. 12)?

C. Why is love greater than faith and hope?

3. Read John 15:5–12.

   A. In what way is Jesus the vine? In what way are we the branches?
   B. What promise is given to those who remain in Jesus (v. 7)?
   C. What happens to the branch that remains in Jesus (v. 8)? Why is this to God's glory?
   D. How do we remain in Christ's love (v. 10)?
   E. What is the result of remaining in Christ's love (v. 11)?
   F. What command does Jesus give those who remain in his love (v. 12)?

Love Given

1. Make a list of the ways others have blessed you through their love. How can you pass along this love to others?

2. In your quiet time, thank God for the many ways he has shown you his love over the years. Be as specific as possible, naming his individual expressions of love. Then ask him to show you how you can better pass along his love to others. Do not conclude your prayer until the Lord has revealed to you several ways in which you can practically show his love to specific individuals in your life.

NOTES

Chapter 2: Love's Flagship
1. David Aikman, *Great Souls: Six Who Changed the Century* (Nashville: Word Publishing, 1998), 341–42.
2. Ibid., 338–44.

Chapter 3: Your Kindness Quotient
1. John 2:1–11; Luke 19:1–10; Mark 5:21–34; Matthew 9:22 NKJV.
2. Gerhard Kittel and Gerhard Friedrich, eds., *Theological Dictionary of the New Testament,* trans. Geoffrey W. Bromiley (Grand Rapids: Eerdmans Publishing Co., 1971), 9:483.

Chapter 4: Inflamed
1. Paul Lee Tan, *Encyclopedia of 7,700 Illustrations* (Rockville, Md.: Assurance Publishers, 1979), 274.
2. Linda Dillow and Lorraine Pintus, *Gift-Wrapped by God: Secret Answers to the Question "Why Wait?"* (Colorado Springs, Colo.: WaterBrook Press, 2002).
3. Hank Hanegraaff, *The Prayer of Jesus* (Nashville, Tenn.: W Publishing Group, 2001), 13–14.
4. My appreciation to Jim Barker for relating this fictional piece.

Chapter 5: God's "No Pecking" Zone
1. Dan McCarney, "Courage to Quit," *San Antonio Express News,* 13 July 2000, sec. 4C.

2. Gerald F. Hawthorne, *Philippians,* vol. 43 of *Word Biblical Commentary* (Waco, Tex.: Word Publishing, 1983), 70.

3. William Barclay, *The Letter to the Romans,* rev. ed. (Philadelphia: Westminster Press, 1975), 164.

Chapter 6: A Call to Common Courtesy

1. King Duncan, *Lively Illustrations for Effective Preaching* (Knoxville, Tenn.: Seven World's Publishing, 1987), 61.

Chapter 7: Getting the "I" Out of Your Eye

1. Gerhard Kittel and Gerhard Friedrich, eds., *Theological Dictionary of the New Testament,* trans. Geoffrey W. Bromiley (Grand Rapids: Eerdmans Publishing Co., 1971), 2:660.

Chapter 8: The Headwaters of Anger

1. Dwight Edwards, *Revolution Within* (Colorado Springs, Colo.: WaterBrook Press, 2001), 57–58.

2. Ibid., 58.

3. Robert Emmit, *Anger Management,* audiotape from a sermon at the Community Bible Church, 2477 East 1604, San Antonio, TX 78232 on 14 January 2001.

Chapter 9: The Heart Full of Hurts

1. Jerry Schwartz, "Where Does One Stash That Trash Ash?" *San Antonio Express News,* 3 September 2000, sec. 29A.

Chapter 10: The Love Test

1. Tim Kimmel, quoted in Stu Weber, *Tender Warrior* (Sisters, Oreg.: Multnomah Books, 1993), excerpted as "Changed Lives," in *A 4th*

Course of Chicken Soup for the Soul (Deerfield, Fla.: Health Communications, 1997), 60–61.

Chapter 11: Love Is a Package Deal

1. Robert J. Dean, *First Corinthians for Today* (Nashville, Tenn.: Broadman Press, 1972), 60.

Chapter 12: A Cloak of Love

1. Gerhard Kittel and Gerhard Friedrich, eds., *Theological Dictionary of the New Testament,* trans. Geoffrey W. Bromiley (Grand Rapids: Eerdmans Publishing Co., 1971), 7:587.
2. John 8:1–11; Matt. 14:22–33; Mark 5:1–20; Matt. 17:24–27.
3. My appreciation to Dr. Harold Wise and Dr. Joe Bob Wise for allowing me to tell their parents' story.

Chapter 13: The Ring of Belief

1. Barbara Bressi-Donahue, "Friends of the Ring," *Reader's Digest,* June 1999, 154.
2. Robert H. Schuller, *The Peak to Peek Principle* (Garden City, N.Y.: Doubleday and Co., 1980), 107.
3. Alan Loy McGinnis, *Bringing Out the Best in People: How to Enjoy Helping Others Excel* (Minneapolis: Augsburg Books, 1985), 32–33.
4. Alan Loy McGinnis, *The Friendship Factor* (Minneapolis: Augsburg Publishing House, 1979), 51–52.
5. David Jeremiah, *Acts of Love* (Gresham, Oreg.: Vision House Publishing, Inc., 1994), 92.
6. Bressi-Donahue, op. cit., 153–60.

Chapter 14: When You're Low on Hope

1. Charles Swindoll, *The Tale of the Tardy Oxcart and 1,501 Other Stories* (Nashville, Tenn.: Word Publishing, 1998), 275.

Chapter 15: He Could Have Given Up

1. My appreciation to J. R. Vassar for this parallel and to David Robinson for allowing me to share it.

2. Deborah Hastings, "Firefighters' Reward: Carrying Son's Body," *San Antonio Express News,* 14 December 2001, sec. 17A.

Chapter 16: Unfailing Love

1. J. I. Packer, *Knowing God* (Downers Grove, Ill.: InterVarsity Press, 1973), 112.

Hope. Pure and simple.

The Teaching Ministry of Max Lucado

You're invited to partner with UpWords to bring radio and the Internet a message of hope, pure and simple, in Jesus Christ!

Visit www.maxlucado.com to find FREE valuable resources for spiritual growth and encouragement, such as:

- Archives of UpWords, Max's daily radio program. You will also find a listing of radio stations and broadcast times in your area.
- Daily devotionals
- Book excerpts
- Exclusive features and presentations
- Subscription information on how you can receive email messages from Max
- Downloads of audio, video, and printed material

You will also find an online store and special offers.

Call toll-free,
1-800-822-9673

for more information and to order by phone.

UpWords Ministries
P.O. Box 692170
San Antonio, TX 78269-2170
1-800-822-9673
www.maxlucado.com

Other *Cure for the Common Life* Products

In the *Cure for the Common Life Workbook*, Max teaches that you are a unique individual, created in God's image, with your own gifts, strengths, and passions. In this exciting companion to the trade book, Max provides practical tools and assessments for exploring and identifying your own uniqueness. He motivates you to put your uniqueness into practice and gives you perspective to redefine "work."

It's never too late to discover your strengths, God's will for your life, or to redirect your career—and cure the otherwise hopeless prognosis of a common life.

Cure for the Common Life Webinar

Visit www.maxlucado.com/discoverthecure to hear directly from Max about *Cure for the Common Life* and to access a helpful tool that takes you on a journey to discover your S.T.O.R.Y.

Listen to the message of *Cure for the Common Life* in your home or take it on the road. This CD makes the perfect gift for the family or friends you know are struggling to find their "sweet spot."

Cure for the Common Life is also available in Spanish

BETANIA

An Angel's Story

Was the birth of Jesus a quietly profound event? Or could it have included heavenly battles, angel armies, and a scheming Satan? Come along as Lucado takes us on a journey into his imagination—pulling back the curtain as we see what might have taken place in *An Angel's Story* (previously titled *Cosmic Christmas*).

And the Angels were Silent

As Jesus entered His final days and faced Golgotha, He acted with loving purpose and deliberate intent. Each step was calculated. Every act premeditated. *And the Angels Were Silent* allows you to enter and observe a revealing and intimate view of our Savior's last week.

The Applause of Heaven

It is what you always dreamed but never expected. It's having God as your dad, your biggest fan, and your best friend. It is having the King of Kings in your cheering section. It is hearing the applause of heaven. Max Lucado believes that the Beatitudes provide what we need to discover the joy of God. Much more than a how-to book on happiness, *The Applause of Heaven* is an encounter with the Source of Joy.

Spanish edition available

COME THIRSTY

Scientists assure us we can't live without water. But survival without God? We sip, we taste, but we often go without a drink from the Lord's well. And we pay the price. We shrink and hearts harden. This life-giving book leads us to the four nutrients needed by every soul. Come to the cross and know your sins are pardoned and your death is defeated. Receive Christ's energy and believe you can do all things through the One who gives you strength. Receive his Lordship, knowing you belong to Him and that He looks out for you. Receive His love and feel confident nothing can separate you from it.

Large Print and Spanish editions available

For an audio/visual presentation and to learn more about *Come Thirsty*, visit www.maxlucado.com/come.thirsty

THE CHRISTMAS CHILD

A Chicago journalist finds himself in a small Texas town on Christmas eve. Lonely and alone, he encounters old faces and new facts . . . a handcarved manger, a father's guilt, a young girl's faith. The trip into the past holds his key to the future, and a scarlet cross shows him the way home.

A GENTLE THUNDER

How far do you want God to go in getting your attention? Don't answer too quickly. What if God moved you to another land? (As He did Abraham.) What if He called you out of retirement? (Remember Moses?) How about the voice of an angel or the bowel of a fish (Gideon and Jonah.) God does what it takes to get our attention. That's the message of this book: the relentless pursuit of God.

Spanish edition available

GIVE IT ALL TO HIM

In this story a woman gives her garbage of shame to the trash man; an old man hands over his heavy bag of regrets. Hundreds walk to the landfill and find it filled with trash.

"You can't live with this," he explains. "You weren't made to."

For individuals and churches, here is a beautiful story of a Savior who can take all our garbage on his shoulders—and amazingly, still stand!

In addition to this story, Max explains in easy-to-understand language what Christ did for us and how to turn in our old baggage and exchange it for new life in him.

For a moving audio/visual presentation of *Give It All to Him,* visit www.maxlucado.com/give.it.all.

THE GREAT HOUSE OF GOD

Using the Lord's Prayer as a floor plan for *The Great House of God,* Max Lucado introduces us to a God who desires his children to draw close to him. Warm your heart by the fire in the living room. Nourish your spirit in the kitchen. Step into the hallway and find forgiveness. No house is more complete, no foundation more solid. So come to the house built just for you, *The Great House of God.*

Spanish edition available

HE CHOSE THE NAILS

Christ's sacrifice has defined the very essence of mankind's faith for the past 2000 years. Now Max Lucado invites you to examine the cross, contemplate its purpose, and celebrate its significance. With his warm, caring style, Max examines the symbols surrounding Christ's crucifixion, revealing the claims of the cross and asserting that if they are true, then Christianity itself is true. The supporting evidence either makes the cross the single biggest hoax of all time, or the hope of all humanity.

Large Print and Spanish editions available

He Did This Just for You

Building on stories and illustrations from the book *He Chose the Nails* by Max Lucado, *He Did This Just for You* is a 64-page evangelistic book that leads the readers through God's plan of salvation and offers an invitation to accept Christ. It's the perfect way to introduce the gospel to friends and acquaintances through Max Lucado's warm and easy to understand writing style. Experience God's grace and plan of salvation for the first time or use this booklet to share the message of hope with someone you know.

Spanish edition available

He Still Moves Stones

Why does the Bible contain so many stories of hurting people? Though their situations vary, their conditions don't. They have nowhere to turn. Yet before their eyes stands a never-say-die Galilean who majors in stepping in when everyone else steps out. Lucado reminds us that the purpose of these portraits isn't to tell us what Jesus *did*—but rather to remind us what Jesus still *does*.

Spanish edition available

A Heart Like Jesus

The heart of Jesus is sacred, and the lessons and examples it provides to us are paramount in our daily mission to follow in His footsteps. Max Lucado poses the question "what if, for one day and night, your heart was replaced by the heart of Christ?" That thought-provoking question leads to many personal revelations demonstrating that we can recast our hearts to be more like that of Jesus.

In the Eye of the Storm

Come face-to-face with Jesus when He experienced more stress than any other day of his life aside from his crucifixion. Before the morning became evening, he has reason to weep, run, shout, curse, praise, and doubt. If you know what it means to be caught in life's storms . . . if you've ever ridden the roller coaster of sorrow and celebration . . . if you've ever wondered if God in heaven can relate to you on earth, then this book will encourage and inspire you.

Spanish edition available

Large Print and Spanish editions available

In the Grip of Grace

Can anything separate us from the love of God? Can you drift too far? Wait too long? Out-sin the love of God? The answer is found in one of life's sweetest words—grace. Max Lucado shows how you can't fall beyond God's love. "God doesn't condone our sin, nor does He compromise His standard. Rather than dismiss our sin, He assumes our sin and incredibly, sentences Himself. God is still holy. Sin is still sin. And we are redeemed."

Just For You

This artistic, full-color book will speak to your heart by combining the incredible images of The Visual Bible movies with the dynamic text of Lucado's classic book, *He Chose the Nails*. Prepare to experience the unmistakable power of the cross as you see how and why Jesus chose to undergo the ultimate sacrifice . . . just for you.

JUST LIKE JESUS

"What if, for one day, Jesus became you?" asks master storyteller Max Lucado. With this simple premise, Lucado tells how God loves you just the way you are, but He refuses to leave you there. He wants you to have a heart like His. He wants you to be just like Jesus.

Large Print and Spanish editions available

JUST LIKE JESUS DEVOTIONAL

This personal month-long journey with the Savior offers Scripture, practical devotions and application sessions to pattern one's life after Christ. Starting at day one, readers meet the Savior and find their way of thinking challenged. As readers begin to think more like Christ, they are challenged to put words into action as the journey escalates into a full force, radical retracing and renewal of what it means to be a follower of Christ.

NEXT DOOR SAVIOR

The universe's Commander in Chief knows your name. He has walked your streets. Endowed with sleepless attention and endless devotion, He listens. The fact that we can't imagine how He hears a million requests as if they were only one doesn't mean He can't or doesn't. For He can and does. There is no person He won't touch. No place He won't go to find you. For even though He is in heaven, He never left the neighborhood. He is near enough to touch. Strong enough to trust. A next-door Savior.

Large Print and Spanish editions available

Hear all about *Next Door Savior* from Max himself at http://www.maxlucado.com/nds.

No Wonder They Call Him Savior

In this compelling quest for the Messiah, best-selling author Max Lucado invites readers to meet the blue-collar Jew whose claim altered a world and whose promise has never been equaled. Readers will come to know Jesus the Christ in a brand-new way as Lucado brings them full circle to the foot of the cross and the man who sacrificed His life on it.

Traveling Light

No wonder we get so weary—we're worn out from carrying excess spiritual baggage. Wouldn't it be nice to lose some of those bags? That's the invitation of Max Lucado. With the twenty-third Psalm as our guide, we learn to release some of the burdens we were never intended to bear. Learn to lighten your load, as Max Lucado embraces what it really means to say, "The Lord is my Shepherd."

Large Print and Spanish editions available

Traveling Light Journal

Dare to slow down, take a break from the chaos of life and commit to meeting Christ like you never thought possible. Find yourself on a 30-day journey, led by Max Lucado, to better understand Psalm 23 and its power to teach you how to lighten your load. Each day includes a Scripture verse, a devotional excerpt, a short prayer, and space to write thoughts and prayers.

WHEN CHRIST COMES

Thoughts of the Second Coming are unsettling. Open graves and occupied clouds. Sins revealed and evil unveiled. Yet, for Max Lucado, the coming of Christ will be "the beginning of the very best." In *When Christ Comes*, Lucado shares how Christians can live in hope, confident in his comfort and peaceful in our preparations for His return.

Spanish edition available

WHEN GOD WHISPERS YOUR NAME

Large Print and Spanish editions available

Do you find it hard to believe that the One who made everything keeps your name on His heart and on His lips? Did you realize that your name is written on the hand of God (Isa. 49:16)? Perhaps you've never seen your name honored. And you can't remember when you heard it spoken with kindness. In this book, Lucado offers the inspiration to believe that God has already bought the ticket with your name on it.

THE CAMPAIGN TO MAKE
POVERTY HISTORY
WWW.ONE.ORG

There is a plague of biblical proportions taking place in Africa right now, but we can beat this crisis, if we each do our part. Step ONE is signing the ONE petition, to join the ONE Campaign.

The ONE Campaign is a new effort to rally Americans—ONE by ONE—to fight global AIDS and extreme poverty. We are engaging Americans everywhere we gather—in churches and synagogues, on the internet and college campuses, at community meetings and concerts. To learn more about The ONE Campaign, go to www.one.org and sign the online petition.

> "Use your uniqueness to take great risks for God! If you're great with kids, volunteer at the orphanage. If you have a head for business, start a soup kitchen. If God bent you toward medicine, dedicate a day or a decade to AIDS patients. The only mistake is not to risk making one."
>
> —Max Lucado, *Cure for the Common Life*

ONE Voice can make a difference.
Let God work through you; join the ONE Campaign now!

This campaign is brought to you by